A Garland of Gold

Lama Jampa Thaye

Series

Ganesha
Press

ABOUT GANESHA PRESS

Ganesha Press is the publishing house of Dechen, an international association of Sakya and Kagyu Buddhist centres and groups founded by Lama Jampa Thaye under the authority of Karma Thinley Rinpoche.

Other books by Lama Jampa Thaye

A Garland of Gold
Diamond Sky
Way of Tibetan Buddhism
Wisdom in Exile
Rain of Clarity
River of Memory: Dharma Chronicles

A Garland of Gold

The Early Kagyu Masters in India and Tibet

Lama Jampa Thaye

RABSEL
PUBLICATIONS

A Garland of Gold : The Early Kagyu Masters in India and Tibet
Copyright © 1990 Ganesha Press Limited

Illustrations by Rana Lister

First printed in the UK by Ganesha Press. This edition by Rabsel Publications in partnership with Ganesha Press and Dechen Foundation Books.

Ganesha Press
121 Sommerville Road, St Andrews, Bristol, BS6 5BX ,UK

Rabsel Publications
16, rue de Babylone
76430 La Remuée, France
www.rabsel.com
contact@rabsel.com

© Rabsel Publications, La Remuée, France, 2022
ISBN 978-2-36017-035-7

Contents

Foreword

༄༅། རྒྱལ་བའི་མཁྱེན་ལྡད་སྤྲུད་དང་། དོན་གཉེར་ཅན་རྣམས་ཀྱི་སྐུན་དུ་ཉུ་རྒྱན། ཞུས་ཕྱོགས་དབྱིན་ཡུལ་རྒྱལ་ཁབ་ཆེན་པོར་བཞུགས་པ་རང་གི་སྐུ་ཚབ། སྔགས་པ་ཇམས་པ་མཐའ་ཡས་ཀྱིས་དེང་དུས་ཐུབ་པ་བསྟན་པ་གྱི་ཉི་མ་ནུབ་ཕྱོགས་སུ་གསར་དུ་ཤར་བའི་སྐབས་བཟང་པོ་འདིར་ཁུ་བ་པའི་ཆེར་དུ། ཁྱབ་བདག་རྡོ་རྗེ་འཆང་ནས། རྗེ་བཙུན་སྒམ་པོ་བའི་བར་དུ་བཀའ་བརྒྱུད་གསེར་པོའི་ཕྲེང་བའི་མཛད་རྣམ་ལྱུང་གསལ་ལྱུན་གསར་བཙུགས། མཛད་འདུག་པ་འདིས། སྤྱིར་སྙབ་དང་རང་རེ་ལུགས་དང་། ཁྱད་པར་བཀའ་བརྒྱུད་བསྐོར་ལ་གསལ་ནུ་འདོང་དོན་གི་གཉེར་ལྱན་པ་རྣམས་ལུ་ཕྲགས་ཕན་གཡོགས་ཡོང་ངེས་པས་ཀྱུན་གྱིས་དེ་ཞིན་གསན་སྟེར་གཏན་པར་ཞུ། སྟེ་ཡོ་ ༡༩༩༠ ཟླ་བ་རྒྱད་པའི་ཚེས་ ༡༥ བཟང་པོ། ཀརྨ་ཕྲིན་ལས་འཞི་མེར་པས་བྲེས།

To those who are interested in and possess faith in Buddha's teaching:

My dharma-regent, Ngakpa Jampa Thaye, who lives in the great western kingdom of England has, at this time when the sun of the Sage's doctrine is newly arising in the West, composed this well-founded history of 'The Garland of Gold' of the Kagyus, from the Lord of Refuge Vajradhara through to Jetsun Gampopa. Since it will certainly be beneficial for those who are interested in the Buddhist tradition in general, and the Kagyus in particular, please listen to it and practise in accord with it.

Written on 15th August, 1990 by the Fourth Karma Thinley.

3

Preface

There is a well-known saying among Kagyus that 'devotion is the head of meditation'. Thus, to inspire devotion towards the glorious Kagyu and as an offering to the lineage, I have compiled this brief account of the early masters of the tradition up to the thirteenth century C.E. together with a selection of their songs on *mahamudra*. Although the lives of some of these masters have been recounted before in English, this is the first time that an account of all the early figures in the tradition has been produced in one volume. This history represents the testament of our lineage forefathers, showing us how they developed devotion and confidence in their gurus, received the inspiration of the *dakini* messengers, obtained the precious lineages, attained the vision of *mahamudra,* and spread the keys to enlightenment. Their songs translated here, though incomplete without a master's textual transmission, offer a connection with the world of *mahamudra.*

My account of the early masters is based on the histories composed by Pawo Tsuklak Trengwa (1504-1566), Go Lotsawa (1392-1481) and Pema Karpo (1527-1592). For various reasons, reliable information on the history of Vajrayana in India and thus on the period of the Indian forefathers of the Kagyu tradition is very fragmentary.

Similarly, though great Tibetan historians such as Pawo Tsuklak and Go Lotsawa have produced generally reliable accounts of the early Tibetan Kagyus, the hagiographies of Marpa and Milarepa, authored by Tsang Nyon Heruka, and the related hagiography of Naropa by Lha'i Tsunpa Rinchen Namgyal, all of which have become famous in the West in translation, are unreliable as historical accounts, being better understood as fictionalized recreations or spiritual-historical novels. As a result, my history of the early Kagyus is much briefer than these biographies might suggest it would be. Furthermore, it is not intended to be exhaustive; I have not utilized all the material in my sources since there are numerous inconsistencies between them. Nor is it intended to be definitive. Rather, my aim in this present work has been to provide a coherent series of short narratives together with some representative works which will serve as an introduction to the early history of the Kagyus.

Some of the material here appeared in a different form in my Ph.D. thesis, but it was not until this summer during a short break from other responsibilities that I actually began writing this book, and it was only after consulting H.E. Jamgon Kongtrul Rinpoche that I decided to complete it. I received the transmissions and teachings of the Kagyu forefathers from Karma Thinley Rinpoche and my other gurus such as Ato Rinpoche and Khenchen Thrangu Rinpoche. Thus, I owe an incalculable debt of gratitude to them.

Ngakpa Jampa Thaye
Anniversary of Lord Gampopa, 6th August, 1990

It is over thirty years since *A Garland of Gold* was published by Ganesha Press. Now it is being re-launched by Rabsel Publications. In the intervening years further material concerning the Kagyu tradition has appeared in various European languages. However, it is my hope that *A Garland of Gold* will still prove valuable as an introduction to the early tradition and its Mahamudra teaching.

I would like to take the opportunity to dedicate this re-publication to the long life of H.H. Karmapa, Trinley Thaye Dorje, supreme head of the Kagyu tradition, and to the flourishing of his dharma activity.

Lama Jampa Thaye
London, 2020

Buddha Vajradhara

Introduction

The Kagyu tradition is one of the four major schools
of Tibetan Buddhism alongside the Sakya, Nyingma
and Gelug. It rose to prominence in the eleventh and
twelfth centuries C.E. some one and a half millenia after
the passing of Lord Buddha. The Kagyu tradition thus
developed during the 'later diffusion' of Buddhism in Tibet,
the 'earlier diffusion' having taken place in the eighth and
ninth centuries through the work of Padmasambhava,
Santiraksita and King Trison Detsun. Since the period of
the later diffusion saw the introduction of a variety of new
tantric cycles from India, the schools which arose at that
time were known as the 'new *tantra*' traditions as opposed
to the 'ancient *tantra*' tradition of the earlier period.

The Kagyu tradition was actually established in Tibet
during the course of the eleventh and twelfth centuries
through the efforts of three successive masters: Marpa the
translator (1012-1097), his student Milarepa (1040-1123),
and the latter's disciple Gampopa (1079-1153). It was from
this last master that the tradition received its full name of
Dakpo Kagyu, since one of Gampopa's alternative names

was Dakpo Rinpoche. This distinguishes it from the Shangpa Kagyu tradition which was transmitted through Khyungpo Naljor (990-1140), disciple of the lady *siddhas* Niguma and Sukhasiddhi. The term 'Kagyu' (*bka' brgyud*) is derived from 'ka-bap zhi-gyu' (*bka' babs bzhi'i brgyud*) meaning 'the lineages of the four pronouncements', which were the lineages of esoteric teachings received and transmitted by Tilopa, Indian patriarch of the nascent tradition.[1]

After Gampopa's death, the Kagyu tradition split into four principal branches: Karma, Baram, Tshal, and Phakmo Dru, from the last of which eight principal subsects subsequently emerged. Under the leadership of the seventeen (to date) incarnations of the Gyalwa Karmapa, the glorious Karma Kagyu branch has been the most extensive of all these, although the Druk, Drikung, and Taklung have also continuously spread the message of the Kagyu to countless beings.

Although the Kagyu tradition began formally in Tibet, its spiritual antecedents lie with the *tantric* masters in India. The six Indian masters who were of particular importance to this tradition were Tilopa and Naropa (the 'close lineage'), and Saraha, Nagarjuna, Sabara, and Maitripa (the 'distant lineage').[2] Marpa the translator, first Tibetan patriarch of the tradition, made a number of journeys to India in the course of which he studied with both Naropa and Maitripa, from whom he received the Six Doctrines of Naropa and the *mahamudra* teachings of the close and distant lineages, respectively.

Mahamudra itself is the ultimate teaching of Vajrayana, transmitted by Buddha Vajradhara, embodiment of the *dharmakaya* itself. According to the **view** of *mahamudra,* although one may look for external causes for the world of appearances, it is mind itself which is the basic ground out of which both *samsara* and *nirvana* originate. As Saraha declares in his *Doha Treasure Song:*

'Mind itself is the one seed of everything
Both *samsara* and *nirvana* flow from it.
To that which, like a wish-fulfilling gem,
Grants all wishes, I prostrate.'[3]

The specific appearances that manifest for us arise through the influence of the imprints of our experience and actions deposited in the continuum of mind, and thus they have no intrinsic reality. Likewise, when the actual nature of mind itself is examined, it is also found to be devoid of the attributes of inherent reality. Possessing no cause from which it might originate, it is free of birth; lacking colour form, shape, or location, it does not endure in the present; lacking any attributes to be destroyed, it is unceasing. Mind's nature is emptiness, since it is free from inherent existence; luminosity, since it is the basis of all appearances; and unceasingness, since this emptiness and luminosity are indestructible.

At the present time, this fundamental nature of mind is obscured in sentient beings by unawareness. This unawareness causes the misapprehension of the natural awareness of mind as a perceiving subject and the natural manifestations of mind's creativity as perceived objects. In this manner, 'mind' and the 'world' are split into two and the dualistic pattern of subject/object, self/other is set. In turn, this establishes the conditions for the development of the emotional defilements such as aggression, passion, and confusion, and ensuing self-centred actions. These defilements and negative patterns of behaviour in turn generate the various forms of life, human or otherwise, in which beings find themselves.

Despite the activity of unawareness, mind's nature is primordially buddha-nature—unceasing luminosity and emptiness. Although surrounded by defilements and neurotic actions, it retains its immaculacy like gold within ore. Enlightenment is therefore already present within mind and need not and cannot be manufactured by any type of spiritual practice. Any effort to produce realization would only further entangle one in dualistic perception, the causal basis of *samsara*. Thus eschewing notions even of removing defilements by antidotes, *mahamudra* **meditation** is simply allowing one's mind to settle by itself in uncontrived naturalness. With this authentic relaxation, the liberating vision of the true nature of mind arises effortlessly.

As Tilopa says:

'Just as the sky relies on no support
So mahamudra has no object.
Relax in the state of uncontrived naturalness.
By loosening your bonds you will attain liberation
    without doubt.'[4]

Mahamudra is expressed in action as a simplicity of attitude and behaviour. Since the world is 'sealed' by the *mahamudra* vision as a sacred realm of infinite depth and possibility, one is not confined by the need to restrict one's actions to consensually created norms. Since the split between self and other is healed in *mahamudra,* unaffected compassion continues to arise spontaneously. *Mahamudra* as **fruit** is the attainment of the state of Vajradhara Buddha, yet even to talk of fruit is misleading, since the nature of mind is primordially Buddha. As such, no new 'fruit' has been brought into being by any 'path' of meditation. In reality, the basis, path, and fruit are one. The fruit is distinguished only by the existence of a recognition of one's buddha-nature mind, which recognition brings about the state of Vajradhara and the endless non-conceptual power of achieving the benefit of all beings.

Tilopa

Naropa

1. The Close and Distant Lineages

The Close Lineage

The 'close' lineage of the Kagyu tradition is the line of teachings received by Marpa from his guru Naropa in India. Although Marpa received *muhamudra* teachings from this master, it is preeminently the 'Six Doctrines of Naropa'—the yogas of heat, illusory body, luminosity, dream, intermediate state, and transference— with which this lineage is associated. The first master in this lineage is Naropa's own guru Tilopa who was born around the middle of the tenth century in Bengal.[5] According to Pawo Tsuklak, while he was still a child, Tilopa had a vision of a *dakini* who told him: 'I Vajravarahi am your mother, Cakrasamvara is your father and you yourself are Vajradhara.' It was not until much later that Tilopa was to understand the significance of this vision.[6]

Tilopa was ordained a *bhiksu* in the monastery of Somapuri and received the name Prajnabhadra. For some years, he engaged in Mahayana studies until he entered Vajrayana through another encounter with a *dakini,* which made him realize the limitations of an over-intellectualized approach to *dharma.* One day while Tilopa was studying a text, he was interrupted by the appearance of a *dakini* in the form of an ugly blue-skinned woman who demanded that he tell her the object of his studies. When he managed to reply that the object was Mahayana philosophy, the hag turned on him with the words: 'In the Mahayana the words are many and the obstacles are many, but in the Vajrayana the words are few and the difficulties are also few.' As soon as the *dakini* had uttered these words, the *mandala* of Cakrasamvara appeared in the sky before Tilopa and the deities of the *mandala* themselves bestowed *abhiseka* upon him.[7]

Tilopa was so devastated by this event that he left the monastery and, in the years that followed, became a wandering yogin, travelling throughout India. From a variety of teachers he received *abhisekas,* textual transmissions and oral instructions comprising the 'four lineages of pronouncement':

1. The pronouncement of *'father-tantra'* handed down through Saraha, Nagarjuna, Aryadeva, Candrakirti, Matangi, Tilopa
2. The pronouncement of *mahamudra* handed down through Saraha, Luyipa, Tengi, Darika, Dakini Sukhadhari, Tilopa
3. The pronouncement of dream and the intermediate state handed down through Dombi, Vinasa, Lavapa, Indrabhuti, Tilopa and
4. The pronouncement of heat handed down through Dakini Sumati, Tanglopa, Shinglopa, Karnaripa, Jalandhari, Krsnacarya, Tilopa.[8]

After some years of meditation, Tilopa was ordered by his guru Matangi to practise the phase of 'action'. During the next twelve years, he remained in Bengal earning a living by pressing sesame, an occupation from which his name 'Tilopa' was derived,[9] whilst by night he worked as a servant for a prostitute. When this twelve year period was over, Tilopa's spiritual insight caused his companions to perceive him in a variety of forms. Some saw him as a blazing mass of fire in the centre of twelve smaller lights. Some saw him as a monk, some as a yogin, while yet others saw him surrounded by a host of young women. To celebrate his realization, Tilopa sang:

'As oil is the essence of sesame
So the natural wisdom is innate.
Although it is in the heart of all beings
It is not realized unless shown by the guru.'[10]

On hearing this the audience was immediately transported to the realm of the *dakinis.*

Empowered by his realization to work for others, Tilopa now travelled throughout India. In the west he defeated a non-Buddhist yogin named Mati in a contest of miracles during which he rode on a lion, controlled the movement of both the sun and moon, and turned his body inside out to reveal the cosmos. In the south, he encountered a theistic philosopher, who had defeated many Buddhist scholars in debate. Unable to withstand Tilopa's power, the philosopher, having converted to Buddhism, applied himself to practice diligently and eventually became a *siddha.* In the east, Tilopa conquered a powerful magician who became his disciple and attained the rainbow body at death. In central India Tilopa converted the barkeeper Suryaprabha by the miracle of changing wine into nectar. In the north, he put an end to a series of murders by converting the criminal who then became his disciple. In Srinagara, he humbled a proud musician, whereupon the latter became his student. Returning once more to the south, Tilopa defeated a materialist philosopher through his explanation of *karma.*[11]

Sometime later a *dakini* revealed to Tilopa that he was now ready to travel to the land of the *dakinis.* She told him that he would require three items in order to ensure the success of his enterprise: a glass ladder, a bridge made of jewels, and a key of sharp grass. Tilopa undertook this quest, without hesitation, arriving at the self-existent palace of Cakrasamvara in the land of Oddiyana where he found his way barred by a group of flesh-eating *dakinis*. Undeterred, he overpowered them using the glass ladder to scale the iron wall that encircled the palace grounds. He then crossed the palace moat on his bridge of jewels. At that point, Tilopa met a second group of *dakinis* who appeared in the guise of low-caste women, yet were in reality the ministers of the Queen herself. Once he had overcome them, Tilopa used his key of sharp grass to enter the palace and gain admittance to the inner sanctum of the Queen of the *dakinis,* Vajrayogini, the *'Dharmakaya* Queen'. Tilopa entered the Queen's *mandala* and she immediately declared: 'You are Cakrasamvara.' Thereupon she bestowed upon him the 'vase', 'secret', 'wisdom', and 'fourth' *abhisekas.* At the moment of each *abhiseka,* he received instruction in the appropriate phase of practice. At the completion of the *abhisekas,* Tilopa had received the transmission of the 'whispered lineage' teachings.[12]

Tilopa had three principal students: Naropa, Riripa, and Kasoripa, but it was Naropa who transmitted the teachings to Marpa Lotsawa, Tibetan founder of the Kagyu tradition, and thus it is Naropa who is the second figure in the 'close' lineage.

Naropa was born in the second half of the tenth century,[13] possibly in Bengal, though some sources claim Kashmir.[14] The son of a royal couple, Kalyanavarman and Srimati, he displayed a religious disposition as a child, but when he reached manhood his parents prevailed upon him to take a wife. His marriage ended in divorce after only eight years. Some say that his wife, Vimala, was the same person as Niguma the great yogini, while others say that Niguma was Naropa's sister.[15]

Having abandoned worldly life, Naropa received ordination from the abbot Buddhasarana and then travelled to Nalanda, the great monastic university in Bihar, where he studied Cittamatra and Madhyamaka philosophy. Complementing this course of textual study, Naropa obtained numerous *tantric* teachings, the most important of which was the Kalacakra cycle from the *siddha* Celupa.[16] In time, he rose to a position of scholarly eminence at Nalanda, eventually being appointed one of the four gate-keepers of the institution. At that time, Naropa was known as Abhayakirti.

It was at that point that Naropa was inspired to abandon his monastery through the blessing of a *dakini*. One day while he was reading a text, a shadow fell over him, and looking up he saw before him an ugly old woman. When the hag questioned Naropa as to what he was reading, he replied that he was reading *sutra* and *tantra*. The old woman then asked him if he understood the true meaning of the text whereupon he replied: 'I understand the words and the meaning.' This answer enraged the hag, who immediately flew into a tantrum and accused him of lying. Naropa, forced to admit the truth of this charge, realized at that the moment that the woman was a *dakini*.

Naropa then asked her who did know the true meaning, to which she replied that the master Tilopa knew it and that he was destined to be Naropa's guru. Naropa realized that he had no choice but to leave Nalanda and find Tilopa. His sudden decision did not meet with the approval of his colleagues and students, who only reluctantly allowed him to depart. In order to prepare himself for this quest, Naropa decided to perform a short retreat dedicated to Cakrasamvara, accomplishing the recitation of the deity's mantra some seven hundred thousand times. Following this retreat, it was revealed to him that his future guru was living in the east and he immediately set out in this direction.

After a long and exhausting search and on the verge of complete despair, Naropa finally found Tilopa who was dressed as a yogin. Tilopa's initial teaching to Naropa took the form of transmission through symbols utilizing twelve objects, each of which symbolized a facet of *mahamudra:* a cotton-cloth, a crystal, a knotted thread, a wish-fulfilling jewel, a jewel at which to gaze, a vase containing water, the sight of many vases of water being poured into one vase and then refilled from that one vase, a matrix of *dharmas,* a snake uncoiling, the guru acting as if dumb, a bindu, and a mirror. As each symbol was shown to him, Naropa instantly intuited its significance as a further revelation of the nature of *mahamudra.* At the conclusion of the transmission, Tilopa confirmed his disciple's understanding. Naropa then entered the period of his apprenticeship known as 'the twelve great austerities'. Over a twelve-year period he endured such tortures as being burned by fire and having sharpened reeds placed under his finger nails, in order to receive a series of twelve instructions of the whispered lineage from his guru:

1. The ordinary wish-fulfilling jewel
2. Attunement
3. Wish-fulfilling jewel of *samaya*
4. Heat
5. Illusory body
6. Dream
7. Luminosity
8. Transference
9. Entering
10. Bliss
11. *Mahamudra*
12. Intermediate state.[17]

At the conclusion of his studies, Naropa received from Tilopa permission to teach. On this occasion, Tilopa predicted that Naropa's foremost disciple would be Marpa the Tibetan, saying,

> 'With the sun of self-liberated wisdom,
> In the monastery of Puspahari
> Dispel the dark ignorance of Mati
> And bathe him in wisdom's brilliance.'[18]

It was some years later at Puspahari near Nalanda that Naropa bestowed the transmission of the lineage on Marpa, giving him the Six Doctrines of Naropa, *mahamudra* and Hevajra. Other significant students of Naropa include the *siddhas* Maitripa, Dombi, Santipa, and the Phamtingpa brothers from Nepal. He bestowed upon the latter the eleven yogas of Vajrayogini which he had received from the goddess herself.[19] Naropa died around the middle of the eleventh century.

Saraha

Sabara

Maitripa

The Distant Lineage

The 'distant' lineage is the lineage of *mahamudra* received by Marpa from Maitripa. There are four masters in this line: Saraha, Nagarjuna, Sabara, and Maitripa himself. Saraha is famed as 'the supreme *siddha* of the new *tantras*.' Most old histories give his date of birth as approximately three centuries after the *parinirvana* of Lord Buddha, but I believe it is more likely that he lived in the eighth to ninth centuries C.E.[20] He was born at Vidarbha into the brahmin caste, hence he is also known as 'the great brahmin'. In his youth, he chose to enter a monastery where he studied the Hinayana teachings. It was some time later that Saraha had an encounter with four brahmin maidens— an encounter that was to lead him to Vajrayana. The maidens urged him to drink four cups of liquor in succession and, complying with their request, he immediately experienced the four joys of the fulfillment stage: 'joy', 'supreme joy', 'beyond joy', and 'simultaneously-arising joy'. In this fashion, the maidens, in reality *dakinis*, bestowed *abhiseka* on Saraha. He subsequently formally entered the Vajrayana through the *abhiseka* of Guhyasamaja, which he received at the monastic university of Nalanda. For a time, Saraha continued to maintain the monastic discipline outwardly, while following the practice of a *tantric* yogin in private. Saraha later took a consort who gave him instructions in her craft of arrow-making and in Vajrayana, and Saraha himself became an arrow-maker. Finally, as a result of his Vajrayana practice, he received the transmission of *mahamudra* from the tenth level *bodhisattva* Ratnamati who had himself received it from Buddha Vajradhara. Saraha expressed his *mahamudra* realization in a number of spiritual songs known as *dohas*[21] and *vajra* songs. The most important of these songs was the trilogy of *dohas* namely, people, king, and queen, which he bestowed upon the inhabitants of the kingdom of Vidarbha. Saraha's two principal students were the *siddhas* Nagarjuna and Luyipa.

He died on the sacred mountain of Sri Parvata in southern India.[22]

The second figure in the distant lineage is the master Nagarjuna, who experienced the supreme realization of *mahamudra* through the teaching of Saraha. He in turn transmitted the lineage of *mahamudra* to Sabara.[23]

Sabara was born into a family of Bengali entertainers sometime in the later part of the tenth century. He was one of three children, having two sisters, and later became a song and dance man, like his parents before him. Sabara met his guru Nagarjuna when the latter was in retreat in Bengal. Although still a child, he requested spiritual instruction. Nagarjuna gave him the *abhiseka* of Cakrasamvara together with detailed instructions on the methods of practice. He then told Sabara that if he practised the meditation of Cakrasamvara and followed the teachings of Saraha's *dohas,* he would achieve recognition of ultimate reality. Finally, Nagarjuna addressed the following injunction to him: '...in the south of India you will be known as the master Sabara, and your sisters will be your consorts.' In accord with this instruction, Sabara entered meditation retreat at Sri Parvata, the last dwelling place of Saraha and there gained full realization of *mahamudra.*[24] His chief disciple was Maitripa.

Maitripa, the last of the four masters of the distant lineage, was born in 1007 C.E.[25] Although his family were brahmins, some time in his youth he began to study *buddhadharma.* His first guru was Naropa, who bestowed upon him the *abhisekas* of Cakrasamvara and Hevajra and urged him to take a consort for the practise of Vajrayana. However, at this time Maitripa rejected Naropa's advice, preferring to concentrate on philosophical studies. Shortly after this, he received ordination as a bhiksu from Santipa at Vikramasila, obtaining the name Maitri in honour of the *bodhisattva* Maitreya.

During Maitripa's years at Vikramasila, the great Atisa

was the master of discipline there. Maitripa was practising the meditation of Vajrayogini, but unfortunately, his use of alcohol as a sacred substance in this meditation led to controversy with the other monks. Atisa's attention was drawn to this and he expelled Maitripa for breaching the *vinaya*. After his expulsion, Maitripa revealed himself to be a *siddha* by floating upon the surface of the Ganges seated upon his meditation-mat. The monks were awe-struck and begged him to stay, but he refused.[26]

Some time later, Maitripa received a command from the *bodhisattva* Avalokitesvara to travel to southern India where he would find his destined guru Sabara. On their first meeting, Sabara appeared as a swineherd accompanied by two women and Maitripa was unable to recognize this apparition as his destined guru. On the second encounter, Sabara appeared before him in a forest in the guise of a hunter of wild boar and, armed with bow and arrow, uttered the following verse:

'In the forest of *samsara's* three realms
Wanders the boar of unawareness,
I shoot the arrow of self-liberated wisdom
And I slay the boar of unawareness
And consume the flesh of non-duality.'

Sabara then vanished only to reappear in the form of a scholar declaring to Maitripa: 'Whatever is unborn is undying.' On hearing these words, Maitripa's doubts and hesitations were destroyed. The apparition of Sabara then faded into space. Subsequently, with the phrase: 'When the guru's words enter one's heart, reality is seen as clearly as treasure in the palm of one's hand,'[27] Sabara bestowed the transmission of *mahamudra* upon Maitripa. Sabara prophesied that Maitripa would finally attain the supreme *siddhi* of enlightenment through the blessing of Vajrayogini.

Maitripa transmitted the *mahamudra* lineage to Marpa Lotsawa, but he also had numerous other students such as Vajrapani to whom he also transmitted *mahamudra* and the Kashmiri scholar Anandakirti to whom he gave the transmission of Maitreya's Uttaratantrasastra.[28]

Marpa

2. The Kagyus in Tibet

Marpa the Translator

Marpa Chokyi Lodro, incarnation of Hevajra and master of the four sets of *tantras,* was born in 1012 C.E. at Chukhyer in the district of Lhodrak, in the southern part of Tsang province. His father was a farmer named Marpa Wangchuk Ozer and his mother's name was Gyalmo Tsho. Marpa's first tutor was a local religious teacher who specialized in the rituals of the eight nagas, but at the age of twelve, Marpa was sent away to study with Drokmi Lotsawa in Myugu Lung. The famed scholar, Drokmi, had studied in both India and Tibet with a number of eminent masters. The most notable of these was Gayadhara, from whom he received the transmission of 'The Path and Its Fruit'.

At the age of sixteen, when he discovered that Drokmi demanded considerable donations for religious teaching, Marpa decided to travel to India to set about acquiring rare *tantric* teachings himself. Later, Marpa said of Drokmi: 'I do not think his kindness was small but great.'[29] Undeterred by his parents' pleas, Marpa exchanged his inheritance for gold and set off. Not wishing to travel alone, he accompanied an older scholar named Nyo Lotsawa who was also engaged in the quest for valuable *tantric* teachings.[30]

Marpa decided to break his journey in Nepal where he could acclimatize himself in preparation for the hot plains of India. During his stay, he studied with Paindapatika and Chitherpa, two Nepali disciples of Naropa, receiving the Hevajra *abhiseka* from Chitherpa. It was from these two masters that Marpa first heard of the greatness of Naropa. The two met for the first time at the *siddha's* residence in Puspahari near Nalanda. Initially, Naropa bestowed upon Marpa the *abhiseka* of Hevajra, together with the textual transmission of the relevant meditation text and accompanying oral instructions. Marpa subsequently adopted Hevajra as his patron deity. Following this, Naropa gave him teaching on the Six Doctrines of Naropa and the rituals of the *dharmapala* Vetali. Naropa then sent him to two other masters, Jnanagarbha and Kukkuripa, for further training. Jnanagarbha bestowed upon Marpa the *abhiseka* of Mahamaya, a *tantra* of the mother-tantra class.[31]

At the conclusion of this first period of training, Marpa returned to Tibet. On arriving back in Lhodrak, he discovered that in his absence his parents had passed away. Therefore, nothing stood in the way of his return to India for further studies except his need for the necessary funds. To finance his next trip, Marpa utilized Naropa's instruction on the propitiation of Vetali by performing ceremonies dedicated to the goddess as a protection-ritual for the sons of wealthy men. As offerings for these ceremonies, he received substantial remuneration in gold. It was at this time that Marpa acquired his first serious students. His own cousin, Marpa Golek, received the *abhiseka* of Hevajra from him.

It was at about the age of thirty that Marpa prepared to venture forth on his second trip to India.[32] Shortly before setting out, he experienced a vision of three *dakinis* who revealed the nature of the lineage of Tilopa and Naropa in a song of symbols:

'The *dakini* sky-flower
Riding on the foal of a barren mare, the whispered
    transmission,
Has scattered the hairs of a tortoise, the ineffable,
And with the stick of a hare's horn, the unborn,
Has awakened Tilopa in the vastness of ultimate
    reality.
Through the mute Tilo, the ineffable beyond speech,
Naro the blind saw ultimate reality.
On the mountain of *dharmakaya*
The lame Mati runs without coming or going.
The dance of the sun, moon and Hevajra
Is the one flavour of the many.
The conch-shell proclaims its fame in the ten
    directions.
It calls out to the strong, who are suitable vessels.
The *cakras* are Cakrasamvara.
Turn the wheel of the *cakras* of the whispered lineage
    without attachment, child.'

Marpa reached Puspahari only to discover that his guru
had departed. He set out immediately to find him and
during his search experienced a series of eight visions.

In the first month, Marpa dreamed of Naropa riding
on a lion accompanied by his two consorts who asked him:
'Are you not bewildered by the illusoriness of dream?'

In the second month, Marpa heard a voice from the
sky urging him to persevere and asking: 'Are you not
bewildered by *samsara*?'

In the third month, Marpa beheld the footprints of
Naropa and heard a voice telling him that his guru's tracks
were as difficult to follow as those of a bird. The voice asked
him: 'Are you not falling into the house of non-existence?'

In the fourth month, Marpa saw a yogin who he thought
might be Naropa. A voice came from the sky, urging him to
loosen the knot of the 'snake of doubt'.

In the fifth month, Marpa thought he had found his guru, who addressed him as follows: 'If you do not recognize the desireless 'rainbow-body' due to the development of desire, how will you understand its meaning?'

In the sixth month, Marpa again believed that he had found his guru. He made an offering of a golden *mandala* to the apparition, but was told that he must offer a *mandala* of ultimate reality.

In the seventh month, Marpa once more thought that he had found Naropa. On this occasion, Naropa ordered him to eat a bowl of brain-matter. When Marpa refused, a voice told him: 'If you do not consume it as great bliss, you will not enjoy great bliss itself.'

In the eighth month, Marpa imagined he saw Naropa but was not sure. He heard a voice telling him he was 'like a deer chasing a mirage.'[33]

When Marpa finally found Naropa, he was so overwhelmed with devotion that he immediately offered him all his gold. The *siddha* threw it all away and, touching the earth with his foot, declared: 'This is all a golden land.' He then bestowed upon Marpa the complete transmission of the twelve instructions of the 'whispered lineage', thus fulfilling the prophecy made by his own guru Tilopa many years previously. At that time, Naropa himself prophesied that Marpa's chief student would be one named Mila. He then declared:

'I prostrate to the being
Known as Thöpaga
Like the sun rising over the snow
In the gloomy darkness of the north.'

When Marpa returned to Tibet at the end of his second visit to India, it was as the spiritual heir of Naropa. Once back in Lhodrak, Marpa married the Lady Dakmedma,[34] bought a farm at Drowolung in his home province of

Lhodrak, and prospered. Shortly afterwards, Dakmedma gave birth to his son and heir, Darma-Dode.

A few years after establishing himself in Drowolung, Marpa paid his third and final visit to India to study with the *siddha* Maitripa.[35] Marpa met Maitripa in eastern India, and although he had already received *mahamudra* from Naropa, it was from Maitripa, heir to the lineage of Saraha, that he obtained the definitive and complete transmission. Marpa himself later declared: 'Through the great venerable Lord Maitripa, I realized the basic essence as unborn and grasped the empty nature of mind. From then on my doubts were removed.'[36] In the years following his return to Tibet, Marpa made two fairly brief trips to Nepal to receive various teachings from a number of masters. Whilst on the return leg of the second of these excursions, Marpa was temporarily detained for a few days in Lisokara in northern Nepal by corrupt customs officials. One night during his stay there, he had an overwhelmingly powerful vision of the *siddha* Saraha who gave him special instructions in *mahamudra*. Marpa subsequently composed 'The *Vajra* Song of the Four Letters' to encapsulate these precepts.

Although, to all outward appearances, Marpa lived the life of a wealthy family man, a considerable number of students sought him out. Of these disciples, four were particularly outstanding, being known as the 'four great pillars': Ngok Choku Dorje, Meton Tshonpo, Tshurton Wangdor, and Milarepa Zhepa Dorje. It was to Milarepa that Marpa bequeathed the 'lineage of practice' consisting of *mahamudra* and the Six Doctrines, and to Ngok Choku Dorje that he transmitted the 'lineage of teaching', consisting of the *anuttara tantra* cycles which he obtained from his gurus in India. Marpa had intended to transmit his lineages through his son, Darma-Dode, but this latter was killed in an accident and was unable therefore to continue his father's lineage.[37] Marpa Chokyi Lodro passed away in 1097 at the age of eighty-six. His wife, Dakmedma, expired simultaneously, her body dissolving into a ball of light and thence into the heart-*cakra* of Marpa. Thus Marpa and Dakmedma were revealed as manifestations of the deities Hevajra and Nairatmya respectively.

Ngok Choku Dorje was born in 1036 at Zhung Riwo into a family originally connected with King Trison Detsun. He initially trained in Nyingma doctrines but later, on hearing the name of Marpa Lotsawa, faith immediately arose in him and he travelled to Drowolung for an audience. When Ngok met Marpa, he offered him a horse. Marpa responded by saying: 'If this is an offering accompanying a request for instruction in the teachings, it is too small, but if it is a request for an interview, it is too large.' Later, when Ngok invited Marpa to his home at Riwo, he offered him seventy black female yaks, a black tent, a dog, a butter-churn, and a pitcher. At that time he received a very extensive range of teaching including the cycles of Hevajra, Catuhpitha, Mahamaya, and the *dharmapala* Vetali. Ngok later said: 'My offerings did not last for more than this.'[38] In time he became a specialist in the *Hevajra Tantra* and maintained Marpa's lineage of teaching.

Ngok Choku Dorje had numerous disciples including Ramtsachen, Bawabachen, Ngok Munpachen, and Sumpa Phodkachen. He passed away at the age of sixty-eight being transported to the realm of the *dakinis.* His lineage continued through his own son, Ngok Dode, born in 1090, who was recognized as a Nyingma incarnation. Ngok's descendants and the succession of his disciples spread the teaching lineage of Marpa throughout Tibet.

Tshurton Wangdor was born in lower Dol, receiving his first spiritual instructions from his father who was a *ngakpa* endowed with great magical power. Like Ngok, on hearing of the power of Marpa, he journeyed to the latter's home to seek an audience. Before Marpa would bestow teaching upon Tshurton, he ordered him to accomplish magical rites against his cousin and enemy Marpa Monnak. Tshurton then entered into retreat to perform the necessary rituals after which he told Marpa that Marpa Monnak could be informed of his impending doom. It came about as predicted that Marpa Monnak was slain by Tshurton's magic. Marpa proceeded to give Tshurton some preliminary instructions[39] and later bestowed upon him the cycle of Guhyasamaja. Tshurton passed this teaching to his own chief disciple, Ronyam Dorje, who hailed from the province of Kham. The followers of Tshurton and his disciples were famous for their teaching of Marpa's Guhyasamaja.

Meton Tshonpo came from the region of Dakpo in southern Tibet. He obtained teachings such as Hevajra from Marpa and passed these teachings to his disciple Zhang Sonamkhar. The disciples who belonged to Meton's lineage concentrated mainly upon the exposition and practice of Hevajra.

Milarepa

Mila the 'Cotton-Clad'

It was Marpa's fourth principal student Milarepa, the 'Saraha of Tibet', incarnation of Manjusrimitra, who followed Marpa as holder of the Kagyu lineage.

Milarepa was born in 1040 C.E., the son of Mila Sherab Gyaltsen and Nyang Za Kargyen, a prosperous couple who hailed from the village of Kya-nga Tsa in Gungthang, western Tibet. His parents named him Thöpaga ('delightful to hear'). Tragedy struck the family when Mila was seven years old. His father died suddenly and, on his deathbed, he entrusted the care of his family and affairs to Mila's paternal uncle and aunt. These relatives proceeded to seize the estate for their own use and pressed Mila, his mother, and sister into humiliating domestic service.

Despite their misfortune, Milarepa's mother endeavoured to ensure that he receive some education. His initial tutor was a Nyingma master named Lotsawa Lanchung, also known as Lu-jaypa. From this teacher, Mila received instruction in meditation on Vajrapani. His mother, it appears, was determined that her son should utilize his intelligence to learn sorcery in order to wreak vengeance on her cruel in-laws. Thus, when Mila reached the age of eighteen, she sent him to Yarlung in Tsang province so that he could acquire the powers of sorcery from the adept Yungton Throgyal, a member of the Nyak clan.

At the conclusion of a year-long apprenticeship with this master, Mila was sent to one of his colleagues named Yeshe Zung, a medical practitioner and sorcerer also known as Lhaje Nubchung, who lived in the village of Khulung in Tsang-rong. This latter gave him instructions in the evocation of the *dharmapala* Rahula. Mila's accomplishment of a retreat dedicated to the propitiation of this deity brought him the required powers of sorcery, and endowed with these, he was able to contrive the death of thirty-five people, relatives and supporters of his aunt and uncle, by causing the latter's house to collapse during a celebration. Mila returned to Yungton Throgyal, his first instructor in sorcery. Having acquired magical methods for the generation of hail storms through a month's meditation retreat, Mila then caused the destruction of the harvest in his native village of Kya-nga Tsa.

It was not long after this last incident that Mila began to feel a strong sense of remorse for his acts of vengeance. A sympathetic Yungton Throgyal advised him that he should seek religious instruction from another Nyingma master named Rongton Lhaga who specialized in *ati-yoga.* Mila followed this advice and received instruction from Rongton, who praised *ati-yoga* to Milarepa saying: 'By practising *ati* one is victorious at the root and at the peak.' However, since Mila was subsequently unable to make any progress despite the power of *ati,* Rongton recommended that he should travel to Lhodrak to meet Marpa Lotsawa, the famous student of the *siddhas* Naropa and Maitripa. While he was receiving this counsel, an unbearable feeling of faith arose in Milarepa, and he set out immediately for Lhodrak. On the night preceding his arrival at Lhodrak, both Marpa and his wife Dakmedma dreamed of Naropa's prophecy that Mila would be Marpa's supreme disciple. The next day, forewarned by his dream, Marpa arranged to be ploughing his fields when his destined student arrived. Coming across Marpa ploughing and drinking beer, Mila was unable to recognize him as his intended teacher. Eventually, Marpa revealed his identity saying: 'I am Marpa Lotsawa.' Milarepa then opened his heart by declaring: 'I am a great sinner from Latod. Please give me the spiritual instructions which lead to buddhahood.'

Marpa gave Mila permission to stay at the farm, but would not bestow any teachings upon him. Instead, Marpa commanded Mila to continue working as a sorcerer for him against his neighbours and enemies. Mila's success in this task so impressed Marpa that he gave him the soubriquet 'Great Sorcerer'. Marpa subsequently ordered Mila to construct a tower on his land. Each time Mila completed his labours, his guru ordered him to pull the tower down and build a new one. This happened on four successive occasions until Marpa allowed the fifth tower to stand. Yet all Mila's labours were in vain, for Marpa persistently refused to impart the teachings. Nevertheless, during this time, he was able to receive instruction on Vajrayogini and *mahamudra* from Marpa's wife Dakmedma and the *abhiseka* of Hevajra from Ngok Choku Dorje. As with the *ati-yoga* precepts, however, Mila was unable to achieve any realization. Having thus, through these great tribulations, purified the great accumulation of evil which he had carried with him from his early life, Mila was finally allowed to receive teachings when Marpa gave him the refuge and *bodhisattva* vows and then led him into the *mandala* of Cakrasamvara. During this *abhiseka*, Mila received the name of Zhepa Dorje ('laughing vajra'} from a host of *dakinis*. Following this, Marpa gave Mila a further series of *abhisekas* including those of Hevajra, Mahamaya, Buddhakapala and Guhyasamaja, finally ordering him to remain in retreat for the next two years. At the end of this period, an offering feast was held in honour of Marpa's own guru Naropa. During the festivities, Milarepa and all the assembled guests actually saw Marpa in the form of Hevajra and Cakrasamvara.

When his studies were over and he had received the practice lineage in its entirety, Mila was sent away by Marpa to enter solitary meditation. Before complying with his guru's command, Mila briefly visited Lama Ngok Choku Dorje, and then travelled on to his own village of Kya-nga Tsa only to discover that his mother had died some time previously. His loss renewed his insight into impermanence and his determination to enter retreat, thus fulfilling the command of his guru.

Mila settled in the cave of White Rock Horse Tooth

near Kya-nga Tsa. After several years of intense austerity, Mila's health began to deteriorate. Fortunately, it was at this point that his sister Peta and an old fiancée, Dzesay, arrived to see him. Alarmed to find Mila in such an extremely weak condition, Peta and Dzesay insisted that he should eat some meat and drink some beer. The food and drink brought restored him to health, but had the unfortunate side-effect of disturbing his meditation. Mila remembered that Marpa had earlier given him a sealed scroll containing advice on problems he might encounter in retreat. On opening the scroll, he discovered detailed instructions in various *hatha-yoga* exercises to dispel just such difficulties. Mila's subsequent practice of heat yoga aided by *hatha-yoga* caused the knot of the *nadis* in the *cakra* of the secret place to untie. Through further practice for another year, the knot of the *nadis* at the *cakra* of the navel was unravelled.[40]

Mila then travelled southwards to the Tingri area, continuing his meditation in a number of caves. There he acquired his first students, Shendormo and the *bhiksu* Sakyaguna. A little while later, Mila went into retreat for the winter on the slopes of the nearby mountain of Lachi. His students feared the worst when he was cut off all winter by exceptionally heavy snow, but the following spring their fears were dispelled when they found him still alive. At the party given by his students to celebrate his return, Mila sang and danced to express the realization he had achieved in retreat. This spontaneous dance itself caused the knots in the *nadis* of the *cakra* at the heart-centre to untie.

Unlike his guru, Milarepa did not take a physical partner for Vajrayana practice since the goddess Tashi Tseringma served as his consort.[41] Milarepa first met this goddess at Chubar Menlung when she manifested herself in wrathful form during his meditation, causing the earth to shake. A host of malevolent demons appeared before him, the most hideous of whom were five flesh-eating demonesses. The chief of these, Tseringma herself, was clashing the sun and moon as cymbals while Milarepa saw forests being shaken, rocks tossed, the sky ablaze and the earth flooded with water. This first encounter was followed by others during which Milarepa was gradually able to subdue Tseringma through the power of his meditative realization. When she finally became his consort, the knots in the *nadis* at Milarepa's throat-*cakra* were untied.

In 1094 C.E., about nine years after he had left Marpa, Milarepa accepted Rechung Dorje Drak as his disciple.[42] Rechungpa was only eleven years old at this time, but was to become one of Milarepa's two chief disciples. Several years after this meeting, Rechungpa was sent by Milarepa to acquire the cycle of 'formless *dakini*' teachings which Marpa had been unable to obtain during his studies in India. Rechungpa successfully received them from the *siddha* Tipupa. On his disciple's return to Tibet, Milarepa was concerned to notice that Rechungpa had grown somewhat arrogant. So, moved by compassion for his erring student, Milarepa performed the miracle of revealing within his own body such deities as Cakrasaṁvara, Hevajra, Guhyasamaja, Catuhpitha, Buddhakapala, and Mahamaya. At that very moment, the *nadis* in the *cakra* in Milarepa's forehead were untied and he became one with all buddhas.

The fame of 'Mila the cotton-clad' gradually spread despite his eremitic life in the forests and mountains of south-west Tibet and northern Nepal. A band of disciples began to form around him, many of whom adopted the white cotton robe, as worn by their master, as the clothing of a yogin. His students were yogins like Drigom Repa, Seban Repa, Repa Zhiwa Od, Ngenton Repa, penitent malefactors like Chira Repa, the former hunter, yoginis such as Selle-od, Rechungma, and Peldarbum, and, most illustrious of all, the 'moon-like' Rechungpa and the 'sun-like' Gampopa. Milarepa passed away in 1123 at the age of eighty-three, going to dwell in the realm of Abhirati, buddha-field of Aksobhya.[43]

Rechungpa ('little cotton-clad one') was born in Gungthang in 1083. His parents named him Dorje Drak ('vajra fame'). When he was just seven years old, his father died suddenly and his mother married his uncle. Five years after his father's death, Rechungpa met Milarepa and, despite his mother's disapproval, he became deeply attached to him, becoming to all intents and purposes, his son. When Rechungpa was fifteen, he contracted leprosy. Fortunately, some travelling Indian yogins took him back with them to India. Once there, Rechungpa obtained instruction in a special meditation of Vajrapani from the master Balacandra which cured his disease.

Rechungpa received *mahamudra* and the Six Doctrines of Naropa from Milarepa. From the *siddha* Tipupa he acquired the 'formless *dakini*' teachings and from the yogini Machik Drubpai Gyalmo he obtained the longevity practice of Amitayus. He also received the transmission of *mahamudra dohas* from the Nepali master Asu. Rechungpa passed away at the age of seventy-seven in 1160 C.E. The holder of Rechungpa's lineage was Geshe Khyungtsangpa (1115-1176) who transmitted the lineage in turn to the yogini Machik Onjo.

Gampopa

Gampopa

Gampopa, the incomparable one from Dakpo, third patriarch of the tradition, was the incarnation of Lord Buddha's disciple Candraprabhakumara whose activity in Tibet was prophesied by Buddha himself.[44] He was born in 1079 in Sewalung in Nyal. His father was Nyiwa Gyalpo, a physician and *ngakpa* and his mother was Shomo Za Checham. Gampopa received medical training from his father and subsequently took up medicine as a career. At the age of twenty-five, he married a young noblewoman who bore him two children, a boy and a girl. His wife and both children perished in an epidemic within a few years of the marriage and Gampopa vowed to dedicate the rest of his life to religious practice. He disposed of his property and set off to find a guru with whom he could study and a monastery where he could receive ordination. Gampopa received ordination as a *bhiksu* at the Kadam monastery of Gya-chak-ri in Phenyul from Geshe Gongkhapa, obtaining the monastic name of Sonam Rinchen. For the next four or five years, he studied and practised under a number of Kadam masters. At lower Dakpo, he obtained the *abhisekas,* textual transmissions and oral instructions of Cakrasamvara, Hevajra, and Guhyasamaja from Geshe Maryul Loden. He also studied Atisa's teachings on 'The Graduated Path of the Three Persons' and related meditational instructions with several masters such as Jayulpa, Nyukrumpa, and Gyayon Dak.

It was during his thirty-second year that Gampopa first heard of Milarepa. One day, Gampopa happened to overhear some beggars discussing the powers of the great yogin. Immediately upon hearing the name Milarepa, he was gripped by a strong wave of emotion. After various auspicious signs had appeared in his dreams indicating the existence of a connection between himself and Mila, Gampopa decided that his future lay in being accepted as Mila's student. He formally requested permission from his

Kadam teachers to make his journey. Geshe Chennawa, famous disciple of Dromten told him: 'You should not abandon our signs,' meaning that he should continue to maintain his observance of monastic rules.

Gampopa found Milarepa in Chu-bar. He presented Mila with gold and a brick of tea as an offering, to which the latter responded by insisting that Gampopa drink half of a skull-cup full of beer. Overcoming his initial reluctance to infringe the *vinaya* in this way, Gampopa accepted and drank the beer, thus proving himself a worthy vessel for the teaching of the *siddhas*. Milarepa questioned him closely about his previous studies, and Gampopa told him that he had received the Guhyasamaja cycle from Geshe Maryul Loden and Hevajra from other Kadam masters. When Gampopa further volunteered the information that he had experienced a meditative absorption lasting thirteen days, Milarepa burst into laughter and exclaimed: 'Butter can never be extracted from sand. Meditate on my heat yoga in order to see the nature of mind.'

After he had accepted Gampopa as his student, Milarepa initially gave him the *abhiseka* of Cakrasamvara and the blessing of Vajrayogini. Having thus ripened him, Mila then gave him teaching on the practice of heat yoga, and direct instruction in the view of *mahamudra*, saying: 'The ultimate view is to look at your own mind. If you seek the view outside the mind, it is like somebody who is already rich searching for wealth.'[45]

Gampopa spent some time familiarizing himself with the techniques he had received from Milarepa. During this period of several months, Gampopa experienced a series of visions induced through the practice of heat yoga and the resulting changes in the *nadis, prana,* and *bindu* of his subtle body. Initially, Gampopa had a vision of the five buddhas of the *mandala*. Milarepa commented: 'This is like a man pressing his eyes and seeing two moons. It has arisen because you have held the five *pranas*. It is neither positive nor negative.' Three months later, Gampopa fainted during a period of meditation when he suddenly envisaged the universe spinning violently. His guru explained to him that this was due to the *pranas* carried in the right and left *nadis* beginning to enter the central *nadi*. Shortly after this occurrence. Gampopa had a vision of the entire sky pervaded by Avalokitesvara. Milarepa explained to him that this signified that the *bindu* was beginning to flow downwards from his crown *cakra*. Gampopa's next vision was a glimpse into the black spot hell. Milarepa merely advised Gampopa to loosen his meditation belt. Some time later Gampopa had another vision, this time one in which he saw the gods raining down nectar, which he alone was able to drink. Milarepa told him that this vision signified that the *bindu* was increasing in the central *nadi* but that he needed to practise some *hatha-yoga* exercises. A month later, Gampopa suddenly experienced a violent and sustained physical trembling. Milarepa advised him to continue with his exercises.

Shortly after this, Gampopa had a vision of the sun and moon being eclipsed. His guru told him that this event signaled that the *pranas* and *bindus* were entering the central *nadi*. The eighth in this succession of spiritual experiences was Gampopa's vision of the *mandala* of red Hevajra. Milarepa connected this with the gathering of the red *bindu* at Gampopa's heart-*cakra*. This vision was followed by a similar experience in which Gampopa saw the *mandala* of Cakrasamvara. This, according to Milarepa, was a token of the *bindu* stabilizing at his navel-*cakra*. Gampopa's next vision, which followed some two weeks later, was of his own body being as vast as space and containing all sentient beings drinking milk. Milarepa informed him that this was a sign that his *pranas* had been transformed into wisdom-*pranas*. A month later, Gampopa saw successively, whilst in meditation, the eight deities of the Bhaisajyaguru cycle, the *sambhogakaya* realms and Sakyamuni as chief of the one thousand buddhas of the fortunate aeon. When he related these visions to Milarepa, his guru said: 'Now you have seen the *sambhogakaya* and *nirmanakaya* buddhas but you have not yet seen the *dharmakaya* buddha.' Milarepa then sent Gampopa to U province to continue his meditation in solitary retreat. He predicted that Gampopa would perceive the *dharmakaya* nature of mind and recognize his guru as being in reality a buddha. He bestowed upon him the name '*Bhiksu* Vajradhara, the one famed throughout Jambudvipa', and ordered him to return on the fourteenth day of the horse month in the year of the rabbit (1123).[46]

Gampopa went first to the Kadam monastery at Sewalung in Nyal, but he soon discovered that his sojourn there was harmful to his *mahamudra* practice. Recollecting Mila's advice, Gampopa entered into retreat for three years until he realized the true nature of mind and simultaneously recognized his guru as truly a buddha. Gampopa then moved to Ode Gungyal where he remained in retreat for a further nine years. By then twelve years had passed since his leave-taking of Milarepa, and he retraced his steps towards his guru's residence in Chubar. At Yarlung, he heard the news of Milarepa's passing and this loss leaving him no alternative, he returned to retreat in Ode Gungyal. A little while later, Gampopa received certain portents that his own life would be threatened by various difficulties. To avert these, he obtained the longevity meditation of White Tara from his old Kadam teacher Geshe Nyukrumpa.

Finally, Gampopa settled in a hermitage in the Gampo hills of southern U province where he began to accept students. In response to the needs of his new disciples, Gampopa established a small monastic complex later to be known as Daklha Gampo, the first monastery of the Dakpo Kagyu. Disciples from all parts of Tibet came to this centre. Gampopa composed many important texts during this period, including *The Jewel Ornament of Liberation* and *The Precious Rosary of the Supreme Path*, both of which display his unification of the two streams of spiritual practice in which he himself had trained: the graduated path teaching of the Kadam tradition and the *mahamudra* teaching of the *siddha* lineage, as transmitted through Milarepa. Unlike the previous masters of the lineage, Gampopa gave *mahamudra* instruction without bestowing an *abhiseka* on the majority, though not all, of his disciples. As Go Lotsawa stated, 'Dakpo Rinpoche produced an understanding of *mahamudra* in those beginners who had not obtained initiations.'[47] This method of teaching became known as *sutra*-tradition *mahamudra*. For Gampopa, its scriptural basis derived from Maitreya's *Uttaratantrasastra*. As he himself told his disciple Phakmo Drupa: 'The basic text of our *mahamudra* tradition is the *Uttaratantrasastra* composed by Lord Maitreya.'[48] Although some great masters have criticized this method, it is better to see it as an expression of Gampopa's great compassion in making *mahamudra,* king of all meditations, available even to those who could not receive or maintain the supremely skillful methods of the *anuttara tantra.*

After extensive labours, Gampopa passed away in his monastery in 1153. On the very day of his death, he gave *mahamudra* teaching to two monks who had come to request Vajrayana *abhiseka.* At the cremation of his body, *dakinis* and gods appeared in the sky and his heart was found intact in the ashes of the pyre.

Four of Gampopa's students, Dusum Khyenpa, Dakpo Gomtsul, Phakmo Drupa, and Baram Darma Wangchuk received the complete transmission of his teaching. These four, directly or indirectly, subsequently became the founding fathers of the 'four major' branches of the Dakpo Kagyu: The Karma, Tshal, Phakmo Dru and Baram. These branches spread Gampopa's *dharma* system of the two streams of Kadam and *mahamudra* throughout Tibet.

The Karma, or as it is sometimes known, the Kamtsang, branch was founded by Karmapa Dusum Khyenpa (1110-

1193), first in the line of the Karmapa incarnations. Dakpo Gomtsul (1116-1169), nephew of Gampopa and heir to the monastery of Daklha Gampo, acted indirectly as the founding patriarch of the Tshal branch, second of the four. It was his student, Zhang Yudrakpa (1123-1193), who actually founded the monastery of Tshal in Gungthang from which this branch spread. The Baram branch was founded by Gampopa's student, Baram Darma Wangchuk, who hailed from the Phenyul area of Tsang. The Phakmo Dru branch, which generated the eight minor lines, was named after Phakmo Dru Dorje Gyalpo (1110-1170). The Phakmo Dru branch itself later ceased to exist as a religious entity, as the practitioners were gradually transformed into politically powerful lay patrons, a process which reached its apotheosis in the establishment in the fourteenth century of Phakmo Dru rule throughout Tibet by Taisitu Jangchub Gyaltsen (1302-1364). The eight minor lines originating with Phakmo Dru's own students were: Drikung, Taklung, Trophu, Druk, Mar, Yel, Shugseb and Yamzang.

Karmapa Dusum Khyenpa

3. The Four Great and Eight Minor Schools

Karma

The Karma Kagyu originated with Karmapa Dusum Khyenpa (1110-1193) (or, as he was also known, Druptop U-se), one of the four main disciples of Gampopa, and incarnation of the *bodhisattva* Avalokiteśvara.

Dusum Khyenpa was born in Tresho in Kham. At the age of sixteen he obtained novice ordination, receiving the name Chokyi Drakpa. Three years later, Dusum Khyenpa travelled to U province where he studied philosophy with the two scholars Jamarpa and Chapa Chokyi Sengge.[49] A little later, Dusum Khyenpa received instruction in Kadam doctrine from Geshe Sharawa.[50] His scholarly studies continued with Patsab, a famed master of *madhyamaka* and Mal Duldzin, a master of *vinaya*. From the renowned Pel Gal-lo and Aseng, two students of Sachen Kunga Nyingpo, Dusum Khyenpa received instruction in the six-limbed yoga of the Kalacakra system.

Dusum Khyenpa's studies with Gampopa commenced with the Kadam graduated path system and then extended to Vajrayana teachings. In addition to these studies with his principal guru, Dusum Khyenpa also received instruction in the Six Doctrines of Naropa from Rechungpa and teachings from Changmo Pangkha, a disciple of Meton Tsonpo. At the conclusion of his training, Dusum Khyenpa was told by Gampopa to enter into meditation in solitude. Following his initial period of practice, Gampopa told him: 'Son, you have severed all connection with *samsara*.' Dusum Khyenpa then continued his intensive practice in Sha'u Takgo until he achieved decisive insight into the inseparability of *samsara* and *nirvana*. He subsequently travelled to Kampo Gangra in Kham, where he established his first monastery. Some time later, he founded a second monastery at Tshurphu in Tolung, which was to become the major monastery of the Karma Kagyus. Dusum Khyenpa was proclaimed 'Karmapa' by the Kashmiri scholar Shakyashri who declared him to be 'the one of buddha-activity' (Karmapa) prophesied in the *Samadhirajasutra*.[51] A black hat woven from *dakinis'* hair which granted liberation to all those who beheld it was bestowed upon him by the *dakinis* themselves.[52]

Dusum Khyenpa's successor as head of the Karma Kagyu was his disciple, Sanjay Rechen, from Yarlung in southern Tibet. While still a child, Sanjay Rechen received teachings from Rechungpa's student, Zangri Repa. He met Dusum Khyenpa at the latter's monastery of Kampo Nenang. Shortly before Dusum Khyenpa died in 1183, he entrusted Sanjay Rechen with special authority over the sect. Subsequently, Sanjay Rechen's own student, Pomdrakpa, was the third master to head the sect. He in turn transmitted authority to his own disciple, Karma Pakshi (1206-1283), whom he recognized as the reincarnation of Dusum Khyenpa. Karma Pakshi received ordination and teachings from the Nyingma master Katok Jampa Bum. After he had travelled and taught in Kham for some time, he spent the next six years at Tshurphu. In 1251, Karma Pakshi received his first invitation to visit China from Prince Kublai, grandson of Genghis Khan. Although this visit and a second subsequent visit were not without difficulties, they contributed greatly to the advancement of Karma Kagyu *dharma*.[53] Karma Pakshi spent his last years back at Tshurphu. He died in 1283, having entrusted his lineage to the yogin Orgyenpa.[54]

Tshal

The existence of the Tshal branch of the Dakpo Kagyu tradition dates specifically from the establishment of a monastery at Gungthang by the *siddha* Lama Zhang. However, since it was Dakpo Gomtsul who was the link between Zhang and Gampopa, it is more correct to trace the development of this sect to him. Gomtsul, the eldest son of Gampopa's elder brother Gyasere and his wife Tsecham, was born in 1116 C.E. At the age of seventeen, he received preliminary ordination from the Kadam master Geshe Ngaripa. This was followed some three years later by full ordination as a *bhiksu*. Having completed his studies at the Shawaling monastery, he joined his uncle, Gampopa, who bestowed upon him the full range of *abhisekas* and instructions. Dakpo Gomtsul then undertook a retreat at Lamphu Sha'u Takgo. In 1151, Dakpo Gomtsul was appointed abbot of Daklha Gampo by Gampopa. Following Gampopa's passing in 1153, Gomtsul supervised some construction work at the monastery and then left for Tolung, north of Lhasa, where he built the new monastery of Tshur Lhalung. Dakpo Gomtsul attracted a large number of followers who flocked from all parts of Tibet to Daklha Gampo and his new establishment at Tolung. He also won the praise of such famous contemporaries as the *madhyamaka* scholar Tsang Nagpa who said: 'Though criticized from afar by unworthy beings, you suppressed one hundred manifestations of pride and arrogance in those who saw you and developed faith in you. I take refuge in the one who possesses merit and brilliance.'[55]

After his death, the abbatial throne of Daklha Gampo passed successively to two more direct students of Gampopa: firstly Gomchung and then Dakpo Duldzin. However, the focus of the tradition's development moved elsewhere with the rise of the various subsects, although Dakhla Gampo remained an important Kagyu monastery in its own right.

Gomtsul's student, Zhang Yudrakpa, figured prominently in this process. Zhang was born in 1123 C.E., the child of a *ngakpa* family. His religious studies began early. As a boy, he studied the *prajnaparamita* with the master Shen, a student of Sachen Kunga Nyingpo, founding father of the Sakyapa school. He also received teachings on Hevajra from Ngok Dode, son and successor to Choku Dorje, Marpa's famous student. His studies extended to the *abhidharma* and *pramana* in which he was trained by Sambu Lotsawa.

At the age of twenty six, Zhang Yudrakpa was ordained by the Kadam teacher Geshe Khargowa. A year later, in 1150 C.E., Zhang met and studied with the scholar Gal-lo, another disciple of Sachen Kunga Nyingpo. From Yerpawa, Zhang received the transmission of the Six Doctrines of Naropa. Thus, when Zhang finally met Dakpo Gomtsul in 1155, he was already well-schooled in both *sutra* and *tantra* and had extensive connections with a number of different lineages. Gomtsul instructed his new student in Gampopa's system of *mahamudra* and Zhang experienced a depth of meditation unknown to him previously. Under Gomtsul's guidance, Zhang deepened his realization by practising the various yogic techniques of the *anuttara tantra.* Having completed his training with his principal master, Zhang dedicated himself to spreading the Kagyu teachings, establishing monasteries and gathering numerous students. His main monastery was located at Tshal Gungthang just south of the city of Lhasa. Due to his wrathful compassion and his powers as a *siddha,*

Lama Zhang dedicated himself to establishing law and order through military means. However, Karmapa Dusum Khyenpa pacified his wrath and brought an end to the disputes in which Lama Zhang was engaged.

Zhang Yudrakpa passed away at the age of seventy in 1193. His successor as abbot of Tshal Gungthang was Shakya Yeshe (1147-1207). For well over a hundred years, the Tshalpa Kagyu was very successful, spreading the doctrine of *mahamudra,* as interpreted by Zhang Yudrakpa throughout Tibet.

Baram

The Baram branch of the Kagyu tradition was initiated by Baram Darma Wangchuk from Phenyul, one of the four principal students of Gampopa. At Daklha Gampo, Barampa received detailed instruction from Gampopa, particularly in the practice of the illusory body, one of the Six Doctrines of Naropa. Later he founded a monastery at Baram in northern Tibet (hence his name Barampa) to which numerous students flocked. Barampa's student, Dromgon Tishri Repa, was one of the greatest figures in the subsequent development of the Baram sect.[56]

Phakmo Dru

The Phakmo Dru branch of the Dakpo Kagyu tradition originated with Gampopa's disciple Phakmo Drupa Dorje Gyalpo (1110-1170). In fact, this branch almost immediately split into a number of subsects and the main branch itself receded in importance. Dorje Gyalpo was born in Kham in 1110. His name and that of the branch come from the place, Phakmo Dru, where he established his monastic seat.

As a young man, he met and studied with some of the most eminent masters of his day, including Chapa Chokyi Sengge with whom he studied *madhyamaka* philosophy. In Sakya, Phakmo Drupa received 'The Path and its Fruit' from Sachen Kunga Nyingpo, the first of his two principal *gurus*. In 1152, he met Zhang Yudrakpa, on whose urging he decided to seek Gampopa at Daklha Gampo. Gampopa subsequently gave him instructions in his own system of *mahamudra,* causing him to achieve complete understanding of all the teachings he had previously acquired. When Gampopa passed away a year later, Phakmo Drupa returned briefly to Sakya, and then having spent some time in Tshal-gang, he finally settled in the Phakmo Dru area of Kham where he remained until his death in 1170. There Phakmo Drupa established a monastery, which was soon remarkably successful in attracting a great number of students, to whom he taught the mixed *mahamudra* and Kadam systems elaborated by Gampopa. Phakmo Drupa gained a reputation among his followers for great saintliness. He received instructions directly from *dakinis* and was able to manifest emanations of his body in twelve different places simultaneously.

The Drikung subsect was founded by Phakmo Drupa's student Drikung Jigten Gonpo, born in Dento Tsondu in 1143 C.E. His parents were both Nyingma practitioners. He met Phakmo Drupa in 1167 and studied with him until the latter's death some two and half years later, following which he performed intensive meditation. Unfortunately, during this period he contracted leprosy but on his sudden cure from this disease, he achieved realization of the 'one flavour' of all phenomena. Jigten Gonpo did not receive ordination until he was thirty-five years old. However, when he later established his own monastery at Drikung in 1179, he maintained a very strict regime. Drikung Jigten Gonpo's fame spread widely and some of his contemporaries, like the Kashmiri scholar Sakyasribhadra, recognized him as an emanation of Nagarjuna. He died in 1217 C.E. at the age of seventy-four. His lineage was maintained by his principal student, Chenna Rinpoche (b. 1175).[57]

The Taklung subsect was established by Taklung Thangpa Tashi Pel (1142-1210), disciple and attendant of Phakmo Drupa. Taklung Thangpa hailed from Yangsho Bongra Teng. In his youth he studied Kagyu *dharma* with Geshe Drakgonpa and received lay ordination at the age of eighteen. Some years later, Taklung Thangpa met Phakmo Drupa. He stayed with his guru for six years in all, receiving the full transmission of the teachings. Following Phakmo Drupa's death in 1170, Taklung Thangpa travelled for some time meeting and studying with, among others, the famed Kadam master Chekhawa. He finally settled in the region of Taklung in 1180 where he was to dwell until his death thirty years later. The Taklung monastery became famous for its strictness; meat and alcohol were totally forbidden After Taklung Thangpa's death, control of the Taklung monastery and the rapidly expanding subsect passed initially to his disciple Rinchen Gon, and hence to Sanjay Yarjon.[58]

The Trophu subsect was founded by the two brothers Rinpoche Gyaltsa (1118-1195) and Kunden Tsangpa Repa (1148-1217), members of a Nyingma family descended from Namkhai Nyingpo of Nub, one of Padmasambava's chief disciples. After studies with numerous masters, the elder brother Gyaltsa met Phakmo Drupa and achieved realization of *mahamudra* In 1171, he constructed a small monastery at Trophu where he was later joined by his younger brother. The most important figure in the early Trophu subsect was Trophu Lotsawa (b.1173), nephew and student of Gyaltsa and Kunden Repa. Although this master studied with a large number of scholars and sages amongst whom were the Indian masters Buddhasri, Mitrayogin, and Sakyasri, he received the transmission of *mahamudra* itself from his uncle, Gyaltsa, and thus continued the lineage of Phakmo Drupa. Following the demise of Trophu Lotsawa, his line was maintained by his son Trophu Sempa Chenpo who was in turn succeeded by Yangtsewa Rinchen Sengge.

The Mar Kagyu subsect was founded by Choje Mar, one of the four close disciples of Phakmo Drupa. This master established a large monastery with two thousand monks at Shogon in Kham. Choje Mar's successors were Mog Chennawa Rinpoche, Sha'u Tsewa, and Nal Rinchen Lingpa. Chosod, a member of this lineage, founded the monastery of Rigya.[59]

The Yamzang Kagyu was based around the monastery of Yamzang, founded in 1206 by Yamzang Choje (1168-1233). Yamzang Choje was a disciple of Phakmo Drupa's student Kalden Yeshe Sengge (d.1207). As a young man, he studied the *vinaya* and Kadam doctrines before meeting Yeshe Sengge in 1198 at the latter's monastery in Zar-ra. Yamzang Choje achieved realization by meditating on Yeshe Sengge's *mahamudra* instructions. Subsequently, he secured the continuation of his master's transmission by founding Yamzang monastery. After Yamzang Choje's death in 1233, his successor as abbot was Rinchen Josay.

The Druk subsect was established by the great master Tsangpa Gya-re (1161-1211) who founded the monastery of Nam-druk in U province, after which the subsect was named. However, the inspirational force behind Tsangpa Gya-re's work was provided by his guru Ling Repa (1128-1188), a direct student of Phakmo Drupa. Ling Repa Pema Dorje was born at Langpo Na in Upper Myang. At the age of seventeen, he received the cycles of Kalacakra, Cakrasamvara, and Yamantaka from the lineage of Rwa Lotsawa. Ling Repa and his consort, the lady Menmo, then studied for some time with Rechungpa's disciple Khyuntsangpa before finally meeting Phakmo Drupa in 1165. When they met, Ling recognized his teacher as a buddha and received the *mahamudra* transmission. At that moment, he achieved direct insight into the nature of mind. Subsequently, Ling was likened to Saraha by Phakmo

Drupa. In his later years, Ling Repa became a successful and wealthy religious teacher, establishing a centre at Namphu where he passed away at the age of sixty in 1188.

Ling Repa's principal disciple was Tsangpa Gya-re Yeshe Dorje of the Gya clan. In his youth, Tsangpa Gya-re studied *abhidharma* with Tathangpa, logic with Kharlungpa, and the *Mahamaya-tantra* with So Darma Senge. He was twenty years old when he met his destined guru, Ling Repa, at Rwalung in Tsang. A short time later, he received meditation instruction from Ling, and after a period of just seven days, his heat yoga practice was so successful that he was permitted to wear the white cotton garment of the Kagyu yogin. For four years until his guru's death in 1188, Tsangpa Gya-re remained at Namphu. He then travelled to Chakphurchen where he remained in retreat for three years, during which time he had a vision of Mahakala, indicating that all obstacles had been removed. During his stay at Chakphurchen, Tsangpa Gya-re also discovered the Sixfold Equal Taste teaching which had been concealed by Rechungpa.[60]

When Tsangpa Gya-re was thirty-two, he received monastic ordination from Lama Zhang Yudrakpa, taking the *bhiksu* name Yeshe Dorje. Prior to his ordination, Tsangpa Gya-re had taken a consort, Kalzang, as advised by his guru, who had himself remained a lay yogin. As well as receiving teachings from Lama Zhang of the Tshal tradition, Tsangpa Gya-re also obtained instructions from Karmapa Dusum Khyenpa. In 1189, Tsangpa Gya-re founded Nam-druk monastery in the Nam valley in U from which the Druk subsect took its name. Tsangpa Gya-re Yeshe Dorje died in 1211. His chief monasteries, Nam-druk and Rwalung, passed to his disciple Sanjay Onre Darma Sengge (1177-1237). From that time on, these monasteries and their affiliated cloisters remained in the control of the Gya clan. This line became known as the Bar ('middle') Druk line.[61]

The two great disciples of Tsangpa Gya-re were Lo Repa (1187-1250) and Gotsangpa (1189-1258), from each of whom two sub-lines of the Drukpa Kagyu developed. Lo Repa met Tsangpa Gya-re when he was sixteen years old. Despite parental objections, he left home to study with his guru and quickly achieved decisive realization. Lo Repa was renowned for his asceticism. In 1241, he founded the monastery of Karpo Cholung, and some time later established the first Druk monastery in Bhutan which he named Tharpa Ling. The line which originated with Lo Repa became known as the May ('lower') Druk.

Tsangpa Gya-re's other principal student, Gotsangpa Gonpo Dorje was born in the Lhodrak area, the home province of Marpa. As a youth, he studied *madhyamaka* philosophy and Kadam doctrine. He met Tsangpa Gya-re at Rwalung and at that time received instruction in *mahamudra* and various other teachings. After Tsangpa Gya-re's death in 1211, Gotsangpa returned to Lhodrak where he practised meditation intensively for a period of three years. Subsequently, he travelled widely in such areas as Mount Kailash and Jalandhara in India, where he met numerous *dakinis.* Like his contemporary Lo Repa, Gotsangpa was famous for the ascetic tenor of his life. His principal students were Orgyenpa (1230-1309) and Yangonpa (1213-1287). The line that originated with Gotsangpa was subsequently styled the To ('upper') Druk.

The Shugseb branch of the Phakmo Dru Kagyu originated with the master Gyergom who was born in Yarlung in southern Tibet in 1144. Gyergom studied with Mal Kawachen, Gampopa's disciple Naljor Chogyung, and Phakmo Dru's disciple Parphuwa, from whom he received the transmission of the *mahamudra* dohas. Subsequently, Gyergom founded the monastery of Nyephu Shugseb, where he was eventually succeeded by his disciple Sanjay On. Thus the cloister gave its name to this subsect.

The Yel branch of the Phakmo Dru Kagyu began with Phakmo Drukpa's student Yelphukpa who founded the monasteries of Jangtsana and Lho Yelphuk.

Songs of the Kagyus

Tilopa's Doha Treasure[61]

Homage to glorious Vajrasattva!
Homage to *mahamudra,* unchanging self-awareness!

The aggregates, elements and sense bases
Arise from and dissolve back into the *mahamudra* nature,
Simplicity, neither existent, nor non-existent.
Beyond the action of mind, it cannot be sought.
In this completely deceptive nature
Since there is no beginning, there is no end.

Whatever occurs in mind's sphere of activity,
It cannot be called the true nature.
This cannot be shown by the guru or received by the
    student.
Do not think of it as mind or non-mind.
By abandoning the many and understanding it as oneness
Attachment to oneness will trap you.

I, Tilo, have no teaching whatsoever.
Neither dwell in solitude nor away from solitude,
Eyes neither wide open nor closed,
Mind neither contrived nor uncontrived.
By realizing that naturalness is not mental activity,
In the simplicity of reality, whatever thought is
    experienced,
When you recognize it as deceptive, just leave it alone,
There is nothing to destroy or preserve, gain or lose.

Don't remain in asceticism in the forest.
Bliss isn't found by bathing and purification.
Liberation isn't gained by worship.
By the realization of no acceptance or rejection,
Authentic self-awareness arises as the fruit.

Once this is attained, there is no need to attend to the path.
Worldly fools may seek this elsewhere,
But by sundering hope and fear, bliss arises.

When mind's self-clinging is pacified,
Dualistic appearances are utterly at peace.
Don't think, imagine, examine,
Meditate, act, or have hope or fear.
When such mental activity is self-liberated,
The primordial nature of reality is attained.

*Thus the Doha Treasure of Tilopa, Lord of Yogins, is completed.
It was translated into Tibetan by the Indian scholar Vairocana
and into English by the layman Jampa Thaye.*

Naropa's Verses of Mahamudra[63]

I prostrate to the great bliss!
To explain *mahamudra:*
All phenomena are one's own mind.
To see an external world is a mental error.
Its essence is empty like a dream.
Mind itself is only the movement of thought.
Natureless, its energy is wind.
Its essence is empty like the sky.
All *dharmas* rest in evenness like space.

That which is termed *mahamudra,*
Can't be pointed out by its essence.
So the real nature of mind
Is the *mahamudra* nature.
In this there is no contrivance or change.
When this reality is experienced
All appearances of the phenomenal world become
    mahamudra,
The great all-encompassing *dharmakaya.*

Relax in natural ease.
Meditate without seeking
The unconceivable *dharmakaya.*
Effort in meditation is mental error.
Just like space and apparitions
Meditation and non-meditation are not two.
From what is it free or not free?
Through such realization by the yogin,
All virtues and sins are liberated.
The defilements are great wisdom,
Friends to the yogin are like the forest to fire.

Where is there to go or stay?
Why meditate in solitude?
Whoever doesn't understand this,

Is only liberated temporarily.
When someone who understands this dies
He dwells in the unwavering state,
No 'practice' or 'non-practice',
No contrivance by antidote, no meditation.

Here nothing is truly existent.
Appearances are naturally liberated in the *dharmadhatu*.
Thoughts are naturally liberated in great wisdom,
The non-dual self-same *dharmakaya*.
Like the current of a great river,
Whatever is done is beneficial.
This is everlasting buddhahood,
The unobjectifiable great bliss beyond *samsara*.

All phenomena are naturally empty.
Clinging to emptiness itself is naturally purified.
No concepts of mental activity,
This is the path of all buddhas.
By the good fortune of these verses of essential
    instructions, may all beings attain *mahamudra*.

*Thus Naropa's Verses of Mahamudra are completed. These
are the words of the master himself. They were translated into
Tibetan by Marpa Chokyi Lodro at Pullahari, and into English
by the layman Jampa Thaye.*

The Doha Treasure Mahamudra Instructions of Sabara[64]

Homage to the great bliss simultaneously arising wisdom
    body!
Existence and non-existence, appearance and emptiness,
The moving and unmoving, the wavering and unwavering,
Throughout the whole of time do not move
From the nature of space.
Although space is termed 'space'
The essence of space is unestablished.
It cannot be shown as is, nor as is-not,
Nor both is and is-not, nor something other than these.
Thus it is beyond objectification.
In this way there is not the slightest distinction
Between space, mind and ultimate reality,
Such distinctions and names are only temporary
    designations,
Meaningless and false expressions.
All *dharmas* are one's own mind.
Not so much as an atom is not included in mind.
Whoever understands primordial non-mind
Discovers the ultimate thought of the Conquerors of the
    three times.

It is known as 'the casket of the *dharma*'.
So it is free from erroneous *dharmas*.
Since its nature is the primordial simultaneously-arising,
It cannot be demonstrated.
As it cannot be expressed, by whom could it be understood?

Only if an owner existed could his property exist.
So that which is, from all eternity, deprived of an owner—
    how could it exist?
Where mind is non-existent, by whom could *dharmas* be
    conceived?
When you seek mind and the appearance of *dharmas,*
Neither they nor the seeker can be found.

Non-existent throughout the three times, neither arising
   nor ceasing,
That which does not change into anything else—
Its true nature is great bliss.
Therefore all appearances are *dharmakaya.*
All sentient beings are buddhas.
All karmic formations are primordially *dharmadhatu.*
All notional *dharmas* are like the horns of a rabbit.

Kye Ho!
When there are no clouds, the suns rays are all-pervasive
But to the blind it is always dark.
The simultaneously arising is all pervasive
But to the confused it is very distant.
Nobody understands non-mind.
Mind is bound by labelling.
Just as a madman possessed by a demon
Suffers helplessly and to no purpose,
So also those caught by the great demon of substantiality
Suffer without reason.
Some foolish ones fettered by discrimination,
Whose lord is at home, search for him elsewhere.
Whatever they do, they do not realize they are deceived.

Kye Ho!
Although the childish don't understand reality
I realize that they do not move from it.
Since I have understood it as without beginning or end,
When it is seen by me, and only I-ness is left,
I do not even see this single one when looking at it.
Since, being without perceiver and perceived, it is ineffable,
Who understands this ineffability?
When ordinary mind was purified
I, the hermit, understood.
The milk of lions is not poured into inferior vessels
And when the roar of a lion is heard in the jungle,

Though the deer are terrified,
The lion cubs rejoice.
Just so, when this primordially unborn great bliss is
    revealed,
The fools with erroneous ideas are frightened,
But the hairs of the worthy bristle with joy.

Kye Ho!
Do not waver in watching mind.
When its nature is understood by itself
Wavering mind dawns as *mahamudra,*
And characteristics are liberated by themselves in great bliss.
Happiness and sorrow are a dream,
Since on awakening they are natureless.
Thoughts of hope and fear are left behind.
Who can conceive of accomplishing or stopping?
Since all *dharmas* of *samsara* and *nirvana*
Are seen as natureless,
And since ideas of expectation or anxiety are totally
    exhausted,
What is there to strive to accept or reject?
All forms and sounds are insubstantial
Like magical illusions, mirages and reflections.
Mind itself, the magician, is like space.
Without centre or edge, by whom can it be recognized?
Just as the Ganges and other rivers
Become one taste in the salt water of the ocean,
So the variety of mind and mental functions
Are recognized to have one taste in the *dharmadhatu.*
Whoever investigates the realm of space
Sees that it is utterly free of centre or periphery.
Likewise when mind and reality are investigated
Not an atom of substance can be found.
When investigated, mind is not perceived.
By not seeing, it is seen.
Just as the crow which has flown from the ship,

After roaming in all directions, returns and settles there,
So though it has followed the desirous mind
Primordial mind settles in the natural state.
Because it is without hope, it is unmoved by conditions.
Because the hiding-place of fear has been destroyed, it is
    the vajra-mind.
When the root is cut, mind is like space.

Kye Ho!
Non-meditation is non-activity of mind.
The natural state of ordinary mind
Is spoilt by contrived concentration.
In naturally pure mind, effort is unnecessary.
Don't hold it nor let it wander but let it rest in itself.
If you do not understand this, meditation is pointless.
By understanding this you transcend meditator and
    meditation-object.
As space is space without fixation
So emptiness is emptiness without meditation.
Non-dual mind is like water and milk.
Everything is the one flavour of continual bliss.
Therefore throughout the three times
Non-activity of mind, the state of unbounded naturalness,
Is what is meant by 'practising meditation'.
Not holding the breath or restraining the mind,
Rest in effortless awareness like a little child.
When a thought arises, just see its nature.
Do not conceive the water and waves to be different.
In the *mahamudra* of non-activity of mind
There is not even an atom upon which to meditate.
Not being separate from non-meditation is the supreme
    meditation.
The flavour of the non-dual simultaneously-arising great
    bliss
Has one taste, like water poured into water.
When it rests in stillness,

Objectifying mind is completely pacified.

Kye Ho!
In the non-dual genuine nature
What is there to accept or reject?
As I myself do not hold or let go any *dharmas*
I don't say anything to you, my son.
Just as a jewel is non-substantial,
The yogin's mind is non-substantial.
Even though he talks about various actions
The yogin's mind is one.
Although it is one, since even its oneness is non-existent,
The variety of forms are rootless.
Like a crazy man without calculation,
Or like a little child, one should act without acting.
The mind arises from the mud of *samsara* like a lotus.
There are no faults to defile it.
Enjoying the pleasures of eating, drinking and making love,
Or afflicting body and mind with suffering,
Whatever you do,
There is nothing to untie or liberate.
With the spontaneous action of realization
When we meet foolish beings,
Tears openly well up from the force of unbearable
   compassion.
Having reversed self and others, their benefit is
   accomplished.
When we examine the benefit, it is free from the three
   objectifications.[65]
It is unreal, like dreams and magical illusions.
Without attachment there is neither rejoicing nor regret.
It is the same as an illusion conjured by a magician.

Kye Ho!
In the primordially pure sky-like nature,
There is nothing whatsoever to abandon nor to attain.

This non-activity of mind is *mahamudra*.
Do not have hopes for the fruit.
Since the mind of expectation never arose in the first place,
What can be abandoned or attained?
If there was something to be attained,
How could the four *mudras* be taught?
Just as deer affected by delusion
Will pursue the water in a mirage,
So with the foolish, affected by desire,
Whatever they seek becomes ever more distant.
There is not the slightest difference whatsoever
Between the primordially unborn and the intrinsically pure.
When the conceptualizing mind is purified in the *dhatu,*
That is called 'Vajradhara'.
Just as a mirage in a desert
Where the appearance of water and the water are not two,
Since it is primordially pure, labelling mind is abandoned,
This is inexpressible as eternity or annihilation.
Like a wishfulfilling gem or tree,
It satisfies aspirations through prayer.
For although the world it is known through conventional
   designation,
In ultimate truth, nothing whatsoever exists.

Thus are completed the Doha Treasure Mahamudra Instructions of Sabara, Lord of hermits. It was translated into Tibetan by the Indian scholar Vairocana and into English by the layman Jampa Thaye.

Lord Marpa Lotsawa's Vajra-Song of 'The Four Letters': The Essence of the Glorious Saraha's Mahamudra Beyond the Activity of Mind[66]

On this glorious and auspicious day of the waxing moon,
The special time of the tenth day,
At the *ganacakra* festival of the *viras*
The son who does not stray from *samaya,*
You, the prince of Logkya, have requested,
'Sing a song not previously heard.'
I have travelled a long way
And my body is overpowered by tiredness.
So this song is not melodious or captivating to the heart.
I am not skilled in poetic composition.
However, because there is noone more important than you,
And I cannot refuse an important man
I will sing a wondrous song which has never been heard
     before,
A song of the thought of the great Brahmin.
You followers of *sutra* and *tantra,* who sit on these seats,
Please listen carefully and consider this in your heart.

In the third month of last spring,
I came up from central Nepal.
After being on the road till lunchtime,
I arrived at the Nepali customs office
In a city of rough people.
As the officials exploit anyone they meet,
Along with other imprisoned Tibetans
I was detained for several days, unable to resist.
One night while dreaming in a light sleep,
Two beautiful brahmin girls,
With marks of noble birth, wearing the sacred thread,
Smiling coyly, and glancing out of the corners of their eyes
Came up to me and said:
'You must go to Sri Parvata in the south!'
I said: 'I have never gone there before

And I do not know the way.'
The two girls said:
'You do not need to do anything difficult.
We shall bear you there on our shoulders.'
They seated me in a palanquin with silk fringes
And lifted it into the sky like a parasol.
Like a lightning flash, in an instant
I dreamed that I reached Sri Parvata in the south,
In the cool shade of a grove of plaksa trees.
On a corpse seat
Sat Lord Saraha, the Great Brahmin.
I had never before gazed upon such splendour face to face.
He was flanked by his two queens.
His body was adorned with the cemetery ornaments.
His joyful face was smiling.

'Welcome, my son!' He said.
Seeing the lord, I felt unbearable joy.
The hairs of my body stood on end, and I could not hold
    back my tears.
I circumambulated him seven times and prostrated to him.
I received the soles of his feet on the crown of my head.
'Father, hold me with your compassion,' I supplicated.

He blessed my body with his.
As he touched the crown of my head with his hand
My body was intoxicated with undefiled bliss.
Like an elephant drunk on beer,
An experience of immovability dawned.

He blessed my speech with his.
By the lion's roar of emptiness,
He uttered the meaning of the 'four letters'.
Like the dream of a mute
An experience of inexpressibility dawned.

He blessed my mind with his.
I realized the meaning of the simultaneously-arising
   dharmakaya.
Beyond coming or going,
Like being in a cemetery
An experience of non-thought dawned.

From the vase of precious song,
The pure speech of vajra-bliss,
With the melody of Brahma and in symbolic speech,
He sang the vajra-song showing the true nature,
The meaning of an empty sky, free from clouds.
Thus I heard this unborn utterance:

Namo!
Compassion and emptiness are inseparable.
The unceasing flow of natural mind
Is primordially pure thusness.
See it like space mixed with space.
Since the root remains at home,
Mind-consciousness is imprisoned.
As you meditate on this,
Nothing is sewn together in the mind.
Recognizing that the phenomenal world is the nature of
   mind,
There is no need for meditation as antidote.
The true nature of mind is beyond thought,
So settle in this uncontrived state.
If you can see this meaning, you will be liberated.
Like a little child, with the behaviour of savages
Eat flesh and be a crazy man.
Be like a fearless lion.
Let the elephant of mind go free.
See the bees hovering among the flowers.
Not viewing *samsara* as wrong,
Nor striving to attain *nirvana,*

The way of ordinary mind
Is to rest in uncontrived nowness.
Do not think of activities.
Do not cling to one side or direction.
Look into the space of unelaboration.'

The exhaustion of *dharmas* is the essential truth,
The summit of views is *mahamudra.*
This symbolic meaning which captures the very essence of
    mind
I heard directly from the Great Brahmin.
At that instant I awoke.
I was caught by the iron hook of this unforgettable
    memory.
Within the prison of unawareness,
I saw the vision of the wisdom of awareness,
Like the sun rising in a cloudless sky,
Clearing the darkness of error.
'Even if I met the buddhas of the three times
I would have nothing to ask them.' I thought.
When this decisive experience of mind arose
Mental functions were exhausted, how wondrous!

E ma! The prophecies of *devatas* and *dakinis,*
And the profound words of the guru,
Although I have been told not to discuss them,
Tonight I cannot help but talk of them.
Except for this very occasion
I have not discussed this before.
Listen with your ears and repeat it later.

I am a man, who has travelled a long way
Without friends or relatives.
Now when my body is weary,
Son, what you have done is in my mind.
I will not forget this, it is held strongly in my mind.

My dear friend, your kindness is repaid.

The lords who dwell above, the gurus,
The bestowers of *siddhi,* the *devatas*
The removers of obstacles, *dharmapalas,*
May these, please, not be angry with me.
May they forgive me if there is any error.[67]

Translated into English by the layman Jampa Thaye.

Jetsun Mila's Root Verses of Illuminating Wisdom[68]

I prostrate to the holy *siddha* gurus!
The lineage of gurus
From the great master Tilopa to the great scholar Naropa
And the translator, Marpa from Lhodrak.

I, the yogin of Gung-thang,
With an attitude of faith
Served the Lhodrak Jetsun.
With compassion he bestowed his thought upon me.
Having obtained his spiritual instructions
I meditated diligently upon them.
When blessing arose
My body blazed with heat,
So I was warm in only a cotton robe.
Luminosity arose in my mind.
Of all the many *tantras* and transmissions, nothing is
    equal to this.
You should know this difference.
When one practises this, the basis, path and fruit arise in
    succession.

Mahamudra is the true nature of mind.
Here, its characteristics will be shown in three parts
Mahamudra as basis, *mahamudra* as path, *mahamudra* as
    fruit.

Mahamudra as basis

It is the thought of buddhas and the mind of sentient beings.
It is without colour, form, centre or periphery.
It is free from bias in any direction.
It cannot be experienced as existent or as non-existent.
It is not deluded and cannot be liberated.
It does not arise from any cause and is not affected by any
    condition.

Wise buddhas cannot contrive it, foolish beings cannot
  damage it.
It cannot be improved by realization nor impaired by error.
In this way, *mahamudra* is the basis.

Mahamudra as path
It is the practice which rests upon the basis.
When settling one settles without objectification.
When resting in stillness one rests without any wavering.
When moving, one moves without holding.
Whatever arises, arises as reality itself.
Whatever is liberated is liberated by itself.
This is the one practice.
In this way *mahamudra* is the path.

Mahamudra as fruit
It is freedom from the liberated,
Freedom from the liberator,
Freedom from hope and fear.
As mind and dharmas are exhausted it is ungraspable.
It transcends mind and expression
In this way *mahamudra* is the fruit.

*In this way, the basis, path and fruit of mahamudra are
explained by Jetsun Milarepa. These instructions were
translated into English by the layman Jampa Thaye.*

Glossary

abhidharma (T. *mngon chos*: higher *dharma*) is the collection
of Lord Buddha's teachings on the constituent elements
of the mental and physical realms. Knowledge of the
abhidharma provides the foundation for penetrating
insight into the inherent emptiness of phenomena. It is
one of the three sections of the Buddhist Canon along
with *sutra* and *vinaya*.

abhiseka (T. *dbang skur*: empowerment, initiation) is the
ritual ceremony in which a *vajra* master leads his student
into the *mandala* of a *tantric* deity, thus conferring upon
him the power to attain realization of that deity. In the
anuttara tantra there are four levels of *abhiseka*, 'vase',
'secret', 'wisdom', and 'fourth'. An *abhiseka* is followed by
textual transmission (T. *lung*) authorizing the student
to use the relevant ritual text and instruction (T. *khrid*)
relating the technique of practice.

anuttara tantra The highest of the four levels of tantra. See tantra.

ati-yoga (T. *rdzogs chen*, also known as *mahasandhi*:
great perfection) is the most important doctrine of the
Nyingma tradition. According to ati, all phenomena

of *samsara* and *nirvana* are primordially empty. Since everything is therefore perfect as it is, buddhahood is attained without need for acceptance or rejection.

bhiksu (T. dge slong). A fully ordained monk

bodhicitta (T. *byang chub kyi sems*: thought of enlightenment). *Bodhicitta* is characterised by the altruistic resolution to attain buddhahood for the benefit of all beings and the application of this resolve in spiritual practice. Ultimately, *bodhicitta* is insight into the fundamental emptiness of all phenomena.

bodhisattva (T. *byang chub sems dpa'*). A being in whom the *bodhicitta* has arisen and who has thus dedicated himself to the achievement of buddhahood in order to achieve the temporary and final well-being of all.

cakra (T. *'khor lo*: circle, wheel). The focal points where the *nadis* of the subtle body converge.

Cakrasamvara (T. *'khor lo bde mchog/'khor lo sdom pa*). A deity of the mother class of *anuttara tantra*, practised in all the new *tantric* traditions but particularly important for Kagyus.

cittamatra (T. *sems tsam*: 'mind-only'). One of the two major Mahayana philosophical schools in India. This school, developed particularly by Asanga and Vasubandhu in the third and fourth centuries C.E. focused upon such *sutras* as *Lankavatara*, which denotes mind as the only basis for the appearance of the phenomenal world.

dakini (T. *mkha' 'gro ma*: sky-goer). A class of female mystic beings who may be divided into three principal categories: (a) the 'simultaneously-born' *dakinis* who are manifestations of the *sambhogakaya* (b) the 'realm-born' *dakinis* who dwell in sacred places located in India and (c) 'mantra-born' *dakinis* who are spiritually realized female *tantric* practitioners.

dharma (T. *chos*: truth, religion). The Buddha's teaching. In *abhidharma* it signifies the elements of existence.

dharmapala (T. *chos skyong*). A class of deity, either transcendental or mundane, whose function is to protect the practitioner from internal and external obstacles. In particular, the transcendental *dharmapalas* embody the four enlightened activities of pacifying, enriching, magnetizing, and destroying.

doha Songs composed by *siddhas* to express and communicate their realization of *mahamudra*.

ganacakra (T. *tshogs kyi 'khor lo*). A feast offering in which desirable aspects of the phenomenal world such as food and drink are offered to the presiding guru or deity and thus integrated into the spiritual path.

Gelug (T. *dge lugs*). The Gelug tradition of Tibetan Buddhism was founded by the great scholar Tsongkhapa Lozang Drakpa (1367-1419 C.E.). The chief characteristics of the tradition are its emphasis on *vinaya*, its adherence to the 'graded path' derived from the Kadam school and to Tsongkhapa's interpretation of *madhyamaka*.

hatha-yoga (T. *'khrul 'khor*) Physical exercises taught by such *siddhas* as Naropa and Virupa and used as an adjunct to the practices of the fulfillment stage of *anuttara tantra*.

Kadam (T. *bka' gdams*). The Kadam tradition originated in the eleventh century C.E. from the teachings of the Indian master Atisa (979-1053) and his Tibetan disciple Dromton (1005-1064). Atisa emphasized the practice of *sutra* and *tantra* in a 'graded path' and also transmitted a series of instructions for meditation on *bodhicitta* known as 'mind-training'. Although to all intents and purposes the Kadam sect ceased to exist after the fourteenth century, its teachings have been preserved by the Kagyu and Gelug schools.

85

Madhyamaka (*dbu ma*: the middle way). The *madhyamaka* is the doctrine of the philosophical school established by Nagarjuna about the beginning of the Christian Era. The central concern of the school is emptiness, realization of which sunders all clinging to the extreme views of eternalism or materialism. Two distinct lines of interpretation arose in India, the Svatantrika and Prasangika.

mahamudra (T. *phyag rgya chen po*: great seal). Generally in the new *tantric* schools *mahamudra* denotes the realization of primordial wisdom attained through the unification of the 'development' and 'fulfillment' stages of *anuttara tantra* practice. In the Kagyu school, *mahamudra* is the meditative accomplishment transmitted from Buddha Vajradhara to Tilopa and Saraha and down to the contemporary holders of the lineage through which one directly settles in and recognizes the nature of mind.

Mahayana (T. *theg pa chen po*: great vehicle). The Mahayana teachings, which stress both the altruistic motivation of *bodhicitta* and the wisdom of emptiness, in contrast to the limited ethical and philosophical outlook of the preceding Hinayana teachings, were originally delivered by Lord Buddha to the *bodhisattva* disciples. The Mahayana began to spread widely from about the first century C.E., a phase which coincided with the public appearance of such Mahayana literature as the *Prajnaparamita* (Perfection of Wisdom) *sutras*.

mandala (T. *dkyil 'khor*). A *mandala* usually refers to the palace of a *tantric* deity, whether constructed, painted or visualized in meditation. In addition, there is a tradition in Vajrayana of offering the entire universe visualized as a *mandala* of total richness to one's guru.

mudra (T. *phyag rgya*: seal). In Vajrayana the term *mudra* most usually signifies hand gestures accompanying various phases of meditation. In addition, Nagarjuna in his

Pancakrama discussed four levels of *mudra: karmamudra, samayamudra, dharmamudra,* and *mahamudra* and their relation to the various stages of *annuttara tantra* practice.

nadis, prana, bindu (T. *rtsa, rlung, thig le*: channels, wind, and seed) comprise the subtle body located within the physical shell. Control of *nadi, prana,* and *bindu* is utilized in such fulfillment stage practices as the Six Doctrines of Naropa.

naga (T. *klu*) are spirits who inhabit watery environments and are often associated with treasure, an association which can extend to spiritual treasure, as in the case of the *Prajnaparamita sutras* which they guarded prior to Nagarjuna's making them public.

ngakpa (T. *sngags pa*, Skt. *mantradhara*). A lay *tantric* yogin. In Tibetan Buddhism many famous *dharma*-masters such as Marpa Lotsawa and Sachen Kunga Nyingpo and numerous Nyingma masters have been *ngakpas* and various *ngakpa* dynastic lineages have flourished.

Nyingma (T. *rnying ma*: ancient ones). The Nyingmas comprise the oldest tradition of Tibetan Buddhism, having their origin in the teachings of the eighth century masters Guru Padmasambhava and Santiraksita. Other great masters who contributed to the development of the tradition include the omniscient Longchen Rabjampa (1308-1363) and Jigme Lingpa (1729-1799). The school consists of both ordained and lay practitioners who follow both the unbroken oral-transmission lineages and the teachings in the 'treasures' composed and concealed most usually by Padmasambhava and subsequently rediscovered and propagated by a predicted 'treasure finder'. The principal teaching in the tradition is *ati-yoga* which represents the pinnacle of the nine vehicle spiritual path maintained by the tradition.

Pramana (T. *tshad ma*). The school of buddhist logic and epistemology developed in India by Dignaga and his follower Dharmakirti.

Sakya (T. *sa skya*). The Sakya tradition takes its name from the monastery founded in Sakya in south-western Tibet in 1073 by Konchog Gyalpo of the Khon clan, an influential family that had previously been Nyingma in affiliation. The Sakya sect was given definite shape by the work of 'the five masters': Sachen Kunga Nyingpo (1092-1158); Sonam Tsemo (1142-1182); Drakpa Gyaltsen (1147-1216); Sakya Pandita (1182-1251); and Chogyal Phagpa (1235-1280). Two subsects. Ngor and Tshar, later developed. The Sakyas are famous as possessors of a vast range of *sutra* and *tantra* teachings but their principal teaching is 'The Path and its Fruit' originally elaborated by the ninth-century Indian yogin Virupa on the basis of the *Hevajra Tantra.* The yogin who practises this cycle in both its preliminary stage 'The Triple Vision' and then its main part 'The Triple *Tantra'* achieves buddhahood through realization of the fundamental inseparability of *samsara* and *nirvana*. The head of the Sakya sect is always drawn from the male line of the Khon family, a tradition which continues to the present day.

samaya (T. *dam tshig*) is the sacred bond of commitment to the guru, deity, and teaching established at the time of receiving *abhiseka,* transmission, or instruction. Although *samaya* is extensive in its remit, covering fourteen basic and eight lesser downfalls, its principal focus is the relationship between guru and student, wherein the latter must maintain his connection to the sacredness of the teaching by unswerving devotion to the guru.

samsara (T. *'khor ba*). The cycle of birth and death, the characteristic of which is suffering and whose origin is unawareness.

siddha (T. *grub thob*: accomplished one). A possessor of *siddhis* is a *tantric* saint who possesses mastery over the phenomenal world as a result of his enlightened insight into its fundamental purity.

Six Doctrines of Naropa (T. *naro chos drug*). The Six Doctrines of Naropa are heat, illusory body, dream, luminosity, transference, and intermediate state. In the yoga of 'heat' (*gtum mo*), the practitioner, through the employment of *hatha-yoga, pranayama* (*srog rtsol*) and visualization, generates a sensation of heat at the navel-*cakra*. With the development of such heat, the yogin gains control over the distribution of *prana* (T. *rlung*: 'wind') and thus experiences a refined state of consciousness. In the yoga of 'illusory body' (*sgyu ma lus*), the yogin learns to arise in the form of a divinity from meditation on emptiness, thus purifying distorted perception. In the yoga of 'dream' (*rmi lam*), the central objective is the recognition of the equivalence of dream and everyday life. By meditating on the yoga of 'luminosity' (*'od gsal*), the yogin recognizes, at the point of falling asleep, the manifestation of the primordial radiance of mind. In the yoga of 'transference' (*'pho ba*), the practitioner acquires the ability to project his consciousness (Skt. vijnana: T. *rnam shes*) to a pure realm (*zhing khams*) at the point of physical death. The last of the six yogas, that of 'the intermediate state' (*bar do*), provides techniques for the attainment of spiritual realization in the intermediate state between death and rebirth. The six doctrines form part of the series of twelve instructions comprising the whispered lineage transmission from Tilopa to Naropa. According to Tilopa's *Chos-drug gi Man-ngag, (gdams ngag mdzod,* vol. *J*), 'heat' derives from the teaching of the *siddha* Carya, 'illusory body' from Nagarjuna, 'dream' from La-va-pa, 'luminosity' from Nagarjuna, 'intermediate state' and 'transference' from the yogini Sukhasiddhi.

sutra (T. *mdo*). The *sutras* are the discourses presenting the Hinayana and Mahayana paths given by Lord Buddha and preserved in the Buddhist Canon. The term *sutra* in Tibetan Buddhism is also used to indicate the non-*tantric* contemplative methods of the 'graded path' to enlightenment introduced by Atisa in his *Lamp of the Path to Enlightenment* which were then absorbed into the various traditions of Tibetan Buddhism.

tantra (T. *rgyud*). The *tantras* are the esoteric teachings presenting the Vajrayana or 'secret *mantra*' path given by Lord Buddha, whether in human or divine form, to His most advanced disciples. The term '*tantra*' indicates the continuum (*tantra*) of the wisdom-mind found in both ordinary beings and Buddhas, which alone makes possible the experience of enlightenment. The inherent wisdom-mind is thus the basis, the path and the fruit of the Vajrayana practice outlined in the *tantras*. In the new *tantric* tradition, four ascending orders or levels of *tantra* are distinguished: *kriya, carya, yoga, and anuttara*. The *anuttara tantra* is further divided into the three classes of 'father', 'mother', and 'non-dual'.

Three Kayas (T. *sku gsum*). The *dharmakaya* (T. *chos sku*) is the ultimate modality of buddhahood: formless, unborn, undying mind. The *sambhogakaya* (T. *long spyod rdzogs pa'i sku*) and *nirmanakaya* (T. *sprul sku*) comprise the means of communicating buddha-wisdom to beings, whether in sacred realms as with the *sambhogakaya* or in the everyday world as with the *nirmanakaya*.

Vajrayana (T. *rdo rje theg pa*). The third and final spiritual vehicle, following Hinayana and Mahayana, which was expounded by Lord Buddha in the *tantras*.

Vajrayogini (T. *rdo rje rnal 'byor ma*) the consort of Cakrasamvara. In her form as Vajravarahi, she is the principal meditation deity utilized at the 'development stage' of *anuttara tantra* by Kagyus. In her form as Naro Dakini, she is one of the most important deities of the Sakya tradition.

vinaya (T. *'dul ba*) is the collection of Lord Buddha's teaching on moral discipline for monks, nuns, and, to a lesser extent, laymen and women. It comprises one of the three sections of the Buddhist Canon.

Index of Phonetic
and Orthographic Transcriptions

The Tibetan proper names and place-names in this book have been transcribed into phonetics for the non-specialist reader. Thus an index of phonetic forms and their orthographic equivalents is provided here

Chogyung	chos gyung
Choje	chos rje
Choku	chos sku
Chokyi	chos kyi
Cholung	chos lung
Chubar	chu bar
Chukhyer	chu khyer
Daklha	dwags lha
Dakpo	dwags po
Darma	dar ma
Dento	ldan stod
Dode	mdo sde
Dorje	rdo rje
Drakgonpa	brag dgon pa
Drakpa	grags pa
Drigom	bri sgom
Drikung	'bri gung
Drokmi	'brog mi
Dromgon	'gro mgon
Dromton	'brom ston
Drowolung	gro bo klungs
Dru	gru
Druk	'brug
Drubpai	grub pa'i
Drupa	gru pa
Druptop	grub thob
Duldzin	'dul 'dzin
Dusum	dus gsum
Dzesay	mdze se
Gal-lo	rgwa lo
Gampo	sgam po
Gampopa	sgam po pa
Gelug	dge lugs
Geshe	dge shes
Go	'gos
Gotsangpa	rgod tshang pa

Golek	mgo legs
Gomchung	bsgom chung
Gomtsul	bsgom tshul
Gon	mgon
Gongkhapa	gong kha pa
Gonpo	mgon po
Gungthang	gung thang
Gungyal	gung rgyal
Gya	rgya
Gyachakri	rgya lcags ri
Gyalmo	rgyal mo
Gyalpo	rgyal po
Nyal	gnyal
Nyiwa	snyi ba
Nyang Za Kargyen	myang za' dkar rgyan
Nyephu	snye phu
Nyingma	rnying ma
Nyingpo	snying po
Nyo	gnyos
Nyon	smyon
Ode	'od de
On	dbon
Onre	dbon ras
Orgyenpa	o rgyan pa
Ozer	'od zer
Pakshi	paksi
Pangkha	spang kha
Parphuwa	spar phu ba
Patsab	pa tshab
Pawo	dpa' bo
Pel	dpal
Peldarbum	dpal dar bum
Pema	padma
Peta	pe ta
Phakmo	phag mo
Phenyul	'phan yul

Phodkachen	phod kha can
Pomdrakpa	spom brag pa
Ramtsachen	ram rtsa can
Rechen	ras chen
Rechungpa	ras chung pa
Repa	ras pa
Rinchen	rin chen
Rinpoche	rin po che
Riwo	ri bo
Rongton	rong ston
Ronyam	ro mnyam
Ronyom	ro snyom
Rwa	rwa
Rwalung	rwa lung
Sachen	sa chen
Sakyapa	sa skya pa
Sambu	sam bu
Sanjay	sangs rgyas
Sempa	sems dpa'
Seban	sa ban
Selle-od	sal le 'od
Sengge	seng ge
Sewalung	se ba lung
Sha'u	sha 'ug
Shangpa	shangs pa
Sharawa	sha ra ba
Shawaling	sha ba gling
Shawu	sha dbu
Shen	gshen
Shendormo	gshen dor mo
Shogon	sho dgon
Shomo	sho mo
Shugseb	shug gseb
So	so
Sumpa	sum pa
Sonam	bsod nams

Takgo	stag sgo
Taklung	stag lung
Tashi	bkra shis
Tathangpa	ta thang pa
Teng	stengs
Thangpa	thang pa
Tharpa	thar pa
Thopaga	thos pa dga
Throgyal	khro rgyal
Tingri	ding ri
Tishri	ti shri
To	stod
Tolung	stod lungs
Trengwa	phreng ba
Tresho	tre shod
Trisong	khri srong
Trophu	khro phu
Tsang	gtsang
Tsangrong	gtsang rong
Tseringma	tshe ring ma
Tsewa	rtse ba
Tshal	tshal
Tshal-gang	tshal sgang
Tshalpa	tshal pa
Tsecham	tshe lcam
Tsho	mtsho
Tshur	'tshur
Tshurton	'tshur ston
Tsondu	gtson du
Tsonpo	tshon po
Tsuklak	tsug lag
Tsurphu	mtshur phu
U-se	dbu se
U	dbus
Wangchuk	dbang phyug
Wangdor	dbang rdor

Yamzang	gya' bzang
Yangonpa	yang dgon pa
Yangsho	gyang shod
Yangtsewa	yang rtse ba
Yarjon	yar byon
Yarlung	yar klungs
Yelphukpa	yel phug pa
Yerpawa	yer pa ba
Yeshe	ye shes
Yudrakpa	gyu brag pa
Yungton	gyung ston
Za	gza'
Zangri	zangs ri
Zar-ra	zwa ra
Zhang	zhang
Zhiwa Od	zhi ba 'od
Zung	gzung

Bibiolography

Tibetan Language Sources

'jam mgon kong sprul ed., *gdams ngag mdzod*, pub. Dingo
Chentze, Delhi, 1979, 17 vols.

karma pa mi bskyod rdo rje et. al., *bka' brgyud mgur mtsho*,
Rumtek, Sikkim, India, n.d.

khams sprul don brgyud nyi ma ed., *do ha mdzod brgyad*,
Tashilong, Palampur, H.P., India, 1973.

*padma dkar po,'brug pa'i chos 'byung published as The Tibetan
Chronicles of Padma dKar-po, Sata-Pitaka Series, Delhi,
1969.*

dpa' bo tsug lag phreng ba, *mkhas pa'i dga' ston*, ed. Lokesh
Chandra, International Academy of Indian Culture,
New Delhi, 1959.

English Language Sources

G.C.C. Chang, *The Hundred Thousand Songs of Milarepa*,
Shambhala, Boulder and London, 1977.

H.V. Guenther

——— *The Life and Teaching of Naropa*, Oxford University
Press, London, 1971.

——— *The Royal Song of Saraha*, Shambhala, Berkeley and
London, 1973.

Lobsang P. Lhalungpa, *The Life of Milarepa,* E.P. Dutton, New York, 1977.

Dan Martin, 'The Early Education of Milarepa', *Journal of the Tibet Society,* Bloomington, 1982.

Hugh Richardson, 'The Karma-pa Sect; An Historical Note', *Journal of the Royal Asiatic Society,* 1958.

G. Roerich trans., *The Blue Annals,* Calcutta: The Asiatic Society, 1953, 2 vols.

Karma Thinley, The History of the Sixteen Karmapas of Tibet, Prajna Press, Boulder, 1980.

Chogyam Trungpa/Nalanda. *The Life of Marpa,* Shambhala. Boulder and London: 1982.

Guiseppe Tucci

——— *Opera Minora II*, G. Bardi, Roma, 1971.

——— *Tibetan Painted Scrolls,* La Libreria Della Stato, Roma, 1949, 3 vols.

Notes

1. It should be mentioned that the Druk subsect of the Dakpo Kagyu have argued that the term bka' brgyud is incorrect and should be replaced by dkar brgyud ('white lineage'). Thus in Pema Karpo's history we find the term dkar brgyud consistently preferred. dkar brgyud alludes to the white (dkar) cotton meditation garment worn by yogins of the tradition.

2. As the names of the *siddhas* vary in form both in Tibetan texts and in western publications I have opted to follow the forms employed by the late doyen of Tibetan studies, Guiseppe Tucci in *Tibetan Painted Scrolls,* Rome 1949.

3. Saraha, *Dohakosa Giti* in 'jam mgon kong sprul (ed.), *gdams ngag mdzod,* vol.7, p. 12.

4. Tilopa, *Mahamudra Upadesa in gdams ngag mdzod, vol. 7, p. 33.*

5. H.V. Guenther. *The Life and Teaching of Naropa,* p. viii, gives Tilopa's date of birth as 988 A.D. However, a consideration of the likely dates of Naropa, the principal student of Tilopa, makes this untenable. See the section on Naropa below.

6. *mkhas pa'i dga' ston,* p. 358.

7. *'brug pa'i chos 'byung,* p. 231.

8. I have utilized here the lists of masters in these lineages provided by Pawo Tsuklak, id., p. 349, rather than the somewhat shorter lists provided by Pema Karpo. In my 'Historical and Theoretical Introduction' to my guru Karma Thinley Rinpoche's *The History of the Sixteen Karmapas of Tibet,* I gave a variant set which was supplied to me by Rinpoche himself.

9. Tilopa's name is spelt variously: thus Tilo-pa, Tilli-pa and Telo-pa but all forms are consistent with the derivation.

10. Pema Karpo, id., p. 234.

11. This sequence of miracles is related by Pema Karpo in *id.,* pp. 236-242.

12. For this account, see *id.,* pp. 245-247.

13. As evidence regarding Naropa's dates, one may note that not only was he the teacher of, and thus senior to Marpa (1012-1097), but he was also the older contemporary of Atisa (979-1053). It is probable, therefore, that Naropa was born sometime in the second half of the tenth century.

14. Pema Karpo, *id.,* p. 251, maintains that Naropa was born in Kashmir. However in the *mkhas pa'i dga' ston* we hear of two views on this subject. Thus, whilst Marpa told his disciple Ngok Choku Dorje that Naropa hailed from Kashmir, in the sub-lineage derived from Rechungpa, Naropa is said to have come from Bengal.

15. H.V. Guenther in *The Life and Teaching of Naropa,* maintains that Niguma was the ex-wife of Naropa but Bokar Rinpoche, meditation master of the Karma and Shangpa Kagyu lineages, told me that she was his sister.

16. Celupa's role in the Kalacakra lineage is alluded to in *The Blue Annals,* p. 755.

17. The accounts of Naropa's apprenticeship in *mkhas pa'i dga' ston* pp. 363-9 and *'brug pa'i chos 'byung*, pp. 253-268, tally in most respects. On these twelve instructions see Naropa, *sNyan-brgyud rDo-rje Tshigs-brkang* in *gdams ngag mdzod*, vol. 7.

18. *'brug pa'i chos 'byung*, p. 267.

19. This teaching reached the Sakya tradition in Tibet during the lifetime of Sachen Kunga Nyingpo (1092-1158), becoming one of the famous 'Thirteen Golden *Dharmas*'.

20. Pawo Tsuklak, *id.*, p. 349, says it was three hundred and sixty years afterwards and Pema Karpo (*'brug pa'i chos 'byung* p. 141) claims it was just three hundred years after the *parinirvana*. H.V. Guenther assigns Saraha to the second century C.E. in his *Royal Song of Saraha*, p. 12.

21. On the meaning of the term *doha*, see H.V. Guenther, *id.*, p 86, note 18.

22. Sri Parvata is located in modern-day Andhra Pradesh. See G. Tucci, *Tibetan Painted Scrolls*, vol 2, p. 617 note 293.

23. See *'brug pa'i chos 'byung*, p. 145 and *mkhas pa'i dga' ston* p. 350. According to tradition, this Nagarjuna and the great Madhyamika Nagarjuna are one and the same. Khenchen Thrangu Rinpoche informed me that it was only in the last hundred years of his six hundred year life that Nagarjuna practised *mahamudra*. However, a number of modern scholars have claimed that there must have been at least two Nagarjunas, one the Madhyamaka philosopher of the first/second centuries C.E. and another later *tantric* master bearing the name. There are also other difficulties: as it is said that Nagarjuna only received and practised *mahamudra* in his sixth century of life, which would be approximately the eighth century C.E., this would mean that his *mahamudra* preceptor Saraha would have to have been alive at that time. Yet we have seen that traditional histories put Saraha several centuries earlier. One might

suggest in possible resolution of this problem that the more correct dating for the distant lineage masters Saraha and Nagarjuna would be in the period from the middle of the ninth to the middle of the tenth centuries. In this way, Saraha and Nagarjuna would be three and two generations, respectively, before Maitripa, last Indian master of the line, whose own dates are well established as 1007-1088 C.E. Nagarjuna, as disciple of Saraha and guru of Sabara, I would suggest should be regarded as an incarnation of Nagarjuna the Madhyamaka master as Guiseppe Tucci has speculated in his *Opera Minora,* p. 210.

24. See the brief account of Sabara in *mkhas pa'i dga' ston,* p. 370 and the somewhat more detailed account in *'brug pa'i chos 'byung,* pp. 146-147.

25. Go Lotsawa, *The Blue Annals,* p. 842.

26. I am following Pawo Tsuklak's account here. Pema Karpo locates this incident later in Maitripa's life, after he had met Sabara.

27. *Saraha, Dohakosa Giti in gdams ngag mdzod, vol. 7, p. 12.*

28. 'jam mgon kong sprul blo gros mtha' yas in *seng ge nga ro,* (p.8A) his commentary on *Uttaratantrasastra,* refers to Maitripa's role in rediscovering and propagating the *Uttaratantrasastra* which had fallen into disuse by the eleventh century C.E. some seven or eight centuries after its original appearance.

29. *Blue Annals, p. 399.*

30. On Nyo Lotsawa see the comments in Hubert Decleer, *'The Melodious Drum Sound All-Pervading',* a paper given at the Fifth International Seminar on Tibetan Studies, Narita, 1989 and drawn to my attention by Dr. Geoffrey Samuel. In this paper, Decleer points out that the rather negative picture of Nyo Lotsawa found in Tsang Nyon Heruka's Hagiography of Marpa is at odds with other more authoritative accounts.

31. Although both the *mkhas pa'i dga' ston,* p. 371 and the *'brug pa'i chos 'byung,* p.438, give this account in *The Blue Annals,* p. 400, it is said that Kukkuripa was a master of the Guhyasamaja and that it was Naropa who gave Marpa the Mahamaya.

32. We can be fairly confident of Marpa's age at this point because Pema Karpo states, id., p. 445, that Marpa met the great Atisa near the Tibet-Nepal border and we know from other sources (e.g. *The Blue Annals,* p. 401) that Atisa entered Tibet in 1042 C.E.. One putative problem is created by the fact that Pema Karpo, like Tsang Nyon, alleges that this encounter with Atisa took place during Marpa's third trip to India, he having paid a second visit to Naropa in the intervening years. However, it is difficult to accept this opinion in view of 1042 C.E. being the date of Atisa's arrival in Tibet, at which time Marpa would be just thirty years old. The notion advanced in the histories of Pema Karpo and Tsang Nyon that by this time Marpa could have completed two very extended sojourns in India and Nepal, married the lady Dakmedma, purchased a farm and acquired three of his major disciples including Ngok Choku Dorje, who was not actually born until 1036, is somewhat unlikely.

33. On these visions, see the *mkhas pa'i dga' ston,* p. 372. *The Blue Annals* omits any reference to visions in its description of Marpa's search, merely confining itself to mentioning that Marpa met Kasoripa. one of Naropa's most important disciples during this time.

34. Both *The Blue Annals,* p.402, and the *'brug pa'i chos 'byung,* p.457, assert that Marpa took a further eight consorts in addition to his principal wife Dakmedma. This would be in harmony with the *mandala* of Hevajra, with which deity Marpa is identified. In this *mandala* the father and mother Hevajra and Nairatmya (T. bdag-med-ma i.e. Dakmedma) have an entourage of eight female goddesses.

35. I am following Go Lotsawa (*The Blue Annals*, p.402) in describing this as Marpa's third visit to India, despite the *mkhas pa'i dga' ston* and *'brug pa'i chos 'byung* assigning Marpa's studies with Maitripa to his initial visit to India. This is difficult to accept for a number of reasons not the least of which is that, since Maitripa was born in 1007 C.E., he was considerably younger than Naropa who did teach Marpa on the latter's first trip to India.

36. *The Blue Annals*, p. 402.

37. In the *'brug pa'i chos 'byung*, p. 457, Pema Karpo mentions the breakage of the lineage of the transference-related technique of 'entering' ('grong 'jug) which Marpa transmitted to Darma Dode. Since Darma Dode was killed in a riding accident before he could transmit it onwards, the lineage was severed. On the occasion of this accident, Darma Dode used the technique to enter and reanimate the corpse of a recently deceased brahmin-boy in India. Hubert Decleer, *op.cit.* has drawn attention to the weighty evidence against Tsang Nyon's claim that Darma Dode predeceased Marpa provided by the *rwa lo tsa ba rnam thar* and Taranatha's *History of Yamantaka,* where it is clearly stated that Darma Dode, though indeed being involved in a fatal horse-riding accident, was actually killed in this way as a result of a religious territorial argument with Rwa Lo, master of Yamantaka, after his father Marpa's decease.

38. *Blue Annals,* pp. 403-4.

39. id., pp. 414-5.

40. Pema Karpo connects the stages of Milarepa's spiritual career with the untying of the knots at the five *cakras* in this way.

41. See *'brug pa'i chos 'byung*, pp. 494-6 for details of Mila's relationship with Tseringma.

42. According to *The Blue Annals*, p. 436.

43. This is according to *'brug pa'i chos 'byung*, p. 498. In Tsang Nyon's hagiography it is asserted that Mila met his death at the hands of a jealous scholar, one Geshe Tsakphuwa, who instigated his mistress to poison Jetsun Milarepa. However this incident is not recounted in the *'brug pa'i chos 'byung* or *The Blue Annals* and thus there are some grounds for doubting its veracity.

44. *As quoted in 'brug pa'i chos 'byung, pp. 511-12, from the snying rje pad ma dkar po'i mdo.*

45. *mkhas pa'i dga' ston*, p. 384.

46. Gampopa's period of training with Milarepa and these visionary experiences are related in the *mkhas pa'i dga' ston*, pp. 384-6.

47. *The Blue Annals*, p.724.

48. As quoted in *'jam mgon kong sprul, seng ge nga ro*, p. 15A.

49. Chapa (phya pa chos seng), a master of the Svatantrika Madhyamaka philosophical school, was also a guru of Sonam Tsemo, second of the five great patriarchs of the Sakya tradition.

50. Sharawa (1072-1142) was a student of Potawa one of the 'three cousins', the major disciples of Dromton, actual founder of the Kadam.

51. *See Karma Thinley, The History of the Sixteen Karmapas of Tibet*, p. 43.

52. *mkhas pa'i dga' ston*, p. 390.

53. For a detailed account of Karma Pakshi's visits to the Mongol court, see Karma Thinley, *op.cit.*, pp. 49-51.

54. On Orgyenpa, see the section on the Druk subsect below and also G. Tucci, *Travels of Tibetan Pilgrims in the Swat Valley*, Calcutta, 1940.

55. *The Blue Annals, p. 465, and mkhas pa'i dga' ston, p. 388.*

56. In later years and down to the present day, the Baram tradition was popular in the Nangchen principality of Kham. The present Baram tulku resides in Bodhnath, Nepal, where a monastery has been established for him.

57. The present heads of the Drikung subsect are Drikung Chetsang, who resides in Ladakh and Drikung Chungtsang who resides in Tibet.

58. The present head of the Taklung subsect is Taklung Shabdrung Rinpoche.

59. The *mahamudra* lineage of the Mar Kagyu was later blended with the *ati-yoga* of the Palyul Nyingma tradition.

60. The sixfold equal taste teaching (T. *ro snyom bskor drug*) comprises techniques of transforming six negativities into wisdom. The six are conceptualisation, defilements, sickness, harm from gods and spirits, suffering, and death.

61. On the Bar Druk line up until Pema Karpo (1527-1592) see *'brug pa'i chos 'byung*, pp. 601-604. After Pema Karpo, the Bar Druk split into the Northern Druk and Southern Druk, the latter being located from that time until the present day in Bhutan. The headquarters of the Northern Druk was, until 1959, the monastery of Sang-ngak Choling north of Mon Tawang, seat of the Gyalwang Drukchen hierarch. The present Gyalwang Drukchen resides in India.

62. In *do ha mdzod brgyad*, pp. 11A-12A.

63. *Phyag rgya chen po tshigs bsdus pa* in *gdams ngag mdzod*, vol.7, pp. 47-48. A guide to this work composed by Jamyang Khyentse Wangpo is also contained in *gdams ngag mdzod*, vol. 7, pp. 48-62. In the *gdams ngag mdzod*, Naropa's root-text is accompanied by an interlinear commentary composed by Shamar Khacho Wangpo (1350-1450). Another edition of this song, mistakenly attributed to Maitripa is found in *do ha mdzod brgyad* pp. 20B-21B.

64. Sabara, *do ha mdzod ces bya ba phyag rgya chen po'i man ngag* in *gdams ngag mdzod*, vol. 7, pp. 28-33. Sabara's song is also found in *do ha mdzod brgyad*, 1B-6B. However, as the order of the verses varies in the two editions, I have followed the order in the *gdams ngag mdzod*.

65. Also known as 'the three circles' i.e. an agent who dedicates a beneficial act, a recipient of this dedication and the beneficial act which is dedicated.

66. *mnga' bdag mar pa lo tsa bas dpal sa ra ha las gsan pa'i phyag rgya chen po yid la mi byed pa snying po don gyi gdams ngag yi ge bzhi pa'i don rdo rje mgur* in *gdams ngag mdzod, vol. 7, pp. 63-66. This song, as contained in the bka' brgyud mgur mtsho has been previously translated into English in the excellent Trungpa/Nalanda, The Rain of Wisdom, pp. 133-137.*

67. Jamgon Kongtrul, in his brief note accompanying Marpa's song in *gdams ngag mdzod* explains that the method of meditation set forth in this song and known as 'The Four Letters' comprises the following stages: (1) 'Severing the root of mind' (2) 'Settling the mind' (3) 'Severing mind's error' (4) 'Transforming error into the path'. Khenchen Thrangu Rinpoche explained the meaning of this to me as follows: the first stage is the experience that occurs when the emptiness of mind is 'pointed out' by the guru; the second stage is settling the mind in this experience of emptiness; in the third stage dualistic perceptions such as viewing *samsara* as intrinsically evil and *nirvana* is inherently positive are destroyed: in the fourth stage all situations are transformed into the spiritual path.

68. Milarepa, *rje btsun mi la'i phyag rgya chen po ye shes gsal byed kyi rtsa ba, in gdams ngag mdzod,* vol. 7, pp. 66-67.

Publishing finished
in January 2022 by Pulsio
Publisher Number: 4016
Legal Deposit: June 2022
Printed in Bulgaria